The Requirements for Activity Based Management

The Requirements for Activity Based Management

The Value of Process

John Bentien

This edition published 2011

Published by lulu.com

Copyright © 2011 John Bentien
All rights reserved

ISBN 9780557126569

Acknowledgements

Thanks have to go to everyone involved in the various iterations of ABM in TSB and Lloyds TSB, particularly the theoretical underpinning from Harry, Colin, Nigel, Phil, and Steve, and the practical development and journey from Duncan, Steve, Chas, Anil and Dave. Their work formed the basis of much of my discussions. Happy Days.

And to everyone who patiently listened and contributed to my ramblings as I developed the approach to, and structure of, my dissertation.

And most importantly to Sylvia, Jennifer and Caroline for their love, support and patience. Thank you.

Contents

What's this book about? 9

What's ABM, and why should we care? 11

The ABM mechanics handbook........................ 93

As seen in Management Accounting 105

A time for reflection 113

Introduction

This book is based around my dissertation submitted in partial fulfilment of the requirements of Sheffield Hallam University for the degree of Master of Science in Business Process Management. It was written in the second half of 1998, and as well as giving me the option to add MSc to my CV, the means to the end also contributed to the discussions at work in how best to marry our process journey with the Activity Based Costing developments in Finance.

My employer was a major Financial Services organisation who was at the forefront of various Business Process Management initiatives in the early to mid nineties (and which has continued to date). Theory and practice were developed and significant improvements were implemented. But mergers and restructures held back the rapid development that could have offered much greater competitive advantage (allegedly).

The dissertation was an attempt to stand back and consider whether our thoughts were right, that the Finance-driven Activity Based Costing needed to be built on a process framework in order to enable a more robust understanding of the business and the requirements for, and impact of, change. We had spent time in the early nineties developing a process framework to understand the business, and it had helped to shape strategic and operational thinking. But had we become so involved in a spiral of theoretical thinking that we were making everything else fit to it? My grandiose idea was that the findings from developing the dissertation would provide a significant input to the decisions being made on the future role of ABM within the organisation.

I can't honestly say they did, but I continued to play some small part in continuing the process journey as Sigma and Lean became the buzz words of a business generation. And every so often, when people asked how we could better understand the end-to-end processes and their associated costs, a few of us would just smile and say "ABM" (but without the pretentious use of quotation marks as we said it). Obviously if the answer is as simple as ABM, then the next question is why wasn't it implemented more widely? And for the (partial) answer to that, read on.....

The Assessor generously described the dissertation as *"A very nice piece of work which has a good academic feel about it but is of genuine practical interest. Well written and presented."* Although hindsight, and a re-reading of the dissertation after several years, ~~possibly~~ probably definitely suggests it is not the defining work that I originally hoped and believed, I hope you find parts of it interesting, informative, and maybe even useful. Although developed and written in 1998 (and please also consider the context in which it was written), I think many of the findings and thoughts still hold true.

Following the reproduction of the dissertation, I have included additional detail on the development of ABM in TSB from 1994/95. This is largely based around the ABM methodology as outlined in the *Guide to ABM* that was developed to provide relevant stakeholders from across the business with an understanding of the what, why and how of gaining innovative management information. This Guide referenced parts of the groundbreaking *BPR in TSB* manual, the foundation of which was some innovative thinking and direction that really was a significant development for a Financial Services organisation at that time.

I have also reproduced an article that appeared in Management Accounting in 2000, reporting on an ABM Knowledge Exchange sponsored by CIMA and hosted by Lloyds TSB. Reading this again after all these years, there are some interesting points that highlight the fundamental practical common sense that was the basis of our ABM development and which is the basis for most improvement approaches that are the flavour of any particular time. The sustainability of those flavours tends to be in the application – the master craftsman doesn't blame his tools.

But now, the Dissertation…..

The Requirements for Activity Based Management

by

John Bentien

January 1999

ABSTRACT

This dissertation identifies the purpose and the factors that enable successful implementation of Activity Based Management (ABM). It examines the extent to which organisations have developed and are using activity based techniques, and in particular whether the underpinning of ABM by other process performance tools and models has an impact on its success.

The development of ABM in Lloyds TSB is presented as a case study to highlight the issues facing implementation. The use of holistic cost and service information, to identify and develop process improvements critical to the delivery of the strategic objectives, differentiated the approach from the narrower scope of much of the published material on ABM, which tends to define it as an extension of Activity Based Costing (ABC). However, after early promise, the perception is that it has largely failed to deliver the significant benefits anticipated. In identifying the requirements, the dissertation also addresses this failure and provides a basis for further development.

Information on the extent to which activity based techniques are used, as well as the support provided for implementation, was gained from questionnaires issued to forty organisations that had declared an interest in ABM and eight others which had a background in process management. The Lloyds TSB experience of ABM was also used to position and compare the research findings. A review of published material covering the requirements for both process management and activity based information supplemented the direct research.

The results highlight discrepancies in definition, application and purpose of activity based techniques, all of which have contributed to a confused discussion of their role and potential benefits. However, the key finding is the significant increase in the scope of benefits claimed from the use of activity based information by organisations that have established a process model. This research indicates that organisations committing to a process perspective, with cross-functional teams and responsibilities, are more likely to exploit ABM to deliver both cost and service benefits.

CONTENTS

Chapter 1
Identifying the Requirements: Background and Objectives   15

Chapter 2
The Development of ABM in Lloyds TSB: A Case Study   23

Chapter 3
The Requirements for Process and Activity Management:
A Review of Published Material   32

Chapter 4
Collecting Experiences of ABM: Research Methodology   43

Chapter 5
Presentation of the Evidence: Research Findings   51

Chapter 6
Requirements and Implications: Discussion of the Findings   61

Chapter 7
Post-Script: The Potential for Further Research   69

References	71
The Questionnaire	75
Questionnaire Results - Base Data	82
Pitfalls in ABM Implementation	90

CHAPTER 1
Identifying the Requirements: Background and Objectives

1.1 Setting the Context

The International Dictionary of Management (Johannsen and Page 1995), which states on its cover that it has *'more than 6000 terms, techniques, concepts of use and interest to business management worldwide'*, has no reference to activity based management (ABM). The Concise Encyclopaedia of Business and Management (Warner 1997) manages two short paragraphs on activity based costing (ABC), which is viewed by many authors as the basis for ABM, but makes no mention of ABM itself.

It could therefore be assumed that a dissertation on the requirements for activity based management offers little significant value, addressing a subject not worth a mention in two major management reference books. This begs the question as to why I have chosen to spend time researching, reviewing and writing this dissertation.

Part of the answer is in a belief that ABM offers the potential of providing the process understanding and information required to enable the necessary action for an organisation to move towards its strategic objectives. This potential was a key driver for the initial implementation of ABM in TSB, and also when it resurfaced following the merger with Lloyds. The potential, however, has not been realised, and understanding the factors that have lead to this 'failure' is one of the key objectives of this work.

The flipside of this understanding of the problems is identifying the requirements that will enable successful implementation. However, as with any management initiative, real success only occurs when it meets its purpose, and understanding this requirement for ABM, in terms of *'why do we need it?'* is the other main objective of this work.

The logical start to a discussion on the requirements for ABM is in defining the term itself. This, however, is a problem as there is no standard textbook definition and the term has been used to cover a wide range of tools, techniques and management practices. Most writers, as discussed in chapter 3, refer to ABM as simply the use of ABC data. The other extreme elicits an emphasis on holistic process measurement and management, as favoured by TSB and discussed in chapter 2. So, to understand the requirements, there is a need to place the development of ABM in the context of the development of other management tools, techniques and practices, in particular the development of process management and activity based costing.

Following discussion of these developments and their role in the requirement for ABM, the remainder of the chapter outlines the need for this dissertation to address the failure of ABM to become more widely accepted, before going on to define the research objectives.

1.2 The Requirement for Process Management

'Companies that organise themselves around core processes do so because they believe process management is as central to corporate strategy as products, markets and other key aspects of their business. But in particular, process competence is seen as essential to performance improvement and vital in terms of delivering superior value to the customer'. (Business Intelligence 1995, p16)

This statement summarises the findings from a review of UK organisations that had implemented process management to address the changing environmental factors that had led to both increased competition and opportunities. As companies were forced to provide a clear focus on their strategic objectives, process management was identified as a key factor in increasing competitive advantage and enhancing shareholder value (Hammer 1991).

Process management requires both a focus on the whole process and an understanding of the links within the process that combine to deliver required value to the customer. As competition intensifies, the need to understand the cost and service dimensions of delivery to the customer becomes more critical and a potential enabler of differentiation.

'Differentiation is likely to be achieved not by one element of the value chain, but by multiple linkages within the value chain. If these linkages can be established, a

sustainable basis of differentiation may well have been found'. (Johnson & Scholes 1993, p39)

Processes that deliver customer requirements inevitably cut across traditional functional boundaries, and the literature (e.g. Hammer 1990) contends that for organisations to be adaptive and flexible enough to respond to the scale of changing environmental factors, there is a need to identify and improve these business processes. Many organisations have moved towards the development of a process based organisation which they hope will better provide the flexibility to meet future strategic objectives, with functional strategies formulated in the context of processes to which they contribute. This development has led to a growing emphasis on the components of process management, and in particular the need for supporting information.

1.3 The Requirement for Process Information

The introduction of process management requires information that reflects a process perspective and enables the setting and prioritisation of process improvement targets. Traditional measurement, mainly focused on the achievement of short term objectives and based on functional or departmental lines, tends to be limited in its value in informing and enabling progress of business strategy. As the individual parts of a business are brought together to complete the process jigsaw, the challenge has been in developing operational measures which allow local control and accountability but which can be framed within the wider process and strategic context.

Process management has implications for the way in which an organisation measures its overall performance. At the most basic level, a concern with processes raises questions about aspects of performance, such as quality and customer service, which may never have been subject to formal or regular measurement before. These new concerns are critical at the operating level where process measures are used to monitor and improve performance.

Much of the focus has been on operational measures, and there has only been scant regard to managerial and support processes. In many organisations, support staff, although a minority in terms of numbers, account for a significant proportion of overall cost. There needs to be a better understanding of the relationship between operational and support processes, to help to identify improvement opportunities and allow the company to progress towards its strategic objectives.

1.4 The Requirement for Activity Information

This section outlines the background to the development of both ABC and ABM as tools to deliver the information required to meet different business needs.

1.4.1 The development of ABC

The development of activity based costing in the late 1980s was seen as addressing the perceived inadequacies of conventional costing. Traditional cost management systems established at departmental level fail to reflect the complexities of the operating environment, focusing on historical inputs rather than the activities which consume resource in producing required output (Johnson & Kaplan 1987).

Classic activity based costing enables a better allocation of resource based on a series of activity drivers, although still primarily based on departments and functions. The limitations with this approach in meeting the process requirement is that the focus is internal, failing to join up the activities that combine to meet the needs of the external customer. It is also built on the premise that reduction in cost is the key to business success and ignores the basic question of *'what does the customer want?'*.

As processes are linked activities, understanding activities is fundamental to effective process management. However, although processes tend to cross functional boundaries in delivering products and services to customers, ABC relies on a hierarchical decomposition of activities within each defined part of the business. This linear thinking has been a fundamental barrier to using ABC as a basis for robust process management.

1.4.2 From ABC to ABM

In 1992, Kaplan recognised the need to focus on using the activity information for more than just costing, when he reflected on his original ideas:

'Five years on, I wish we could rename the baby. It's about more than activities, and more than costing: it's about management'. (Kaplan 1992, p.6)

The distinction between ABC and ABM tends to be stated in terms of delivery and use of costing information. The information provided through ABC has been used to enable better understanding of product and customer profitability. ABM, from a financial perspective, takes this information to identify cost and profitability improvement opportunities. However, most writers (as discussed in chapter 3), fail to identify the potential of extending the activity based information, in terms of both scope and usage, to the process requirements.

1.5 The Failure of ABM

For most organisations, activity based techniques remain an untried foundation for management information, and so remain tainted with uncertainty. Awareness has increased in recent years, focused on its application for understanding and managing costs. However, surveys have shown that while there is a growing recognition of the weaknesses of conventional approaches to costing and cost management, there is also a great reluctance to do anything about it, mainly through a cultural resistance to change. (Develin & Bellis-Jones 1995). It is not surprising therefore that there is a reluctance in organisations to use activity based techniques as part of a suite of tools to understand and improve cross functional processes.

The Employers' Group of the Chartered Institute of Management Accountants (CIMA) has organised a number of ABM Exchanges for companies stating an interest, however vague or committed, in activity based management. Findings from these events indicated two common factors that had reduced the impact of ABM programmes: the inability to demonstrate any cost benefit; and the retention of traditional cost management systems.

There was also evidence of the impact of differences in approaches to implementation between different types of organisation. In non-manufacturing organisations there was clear evidence of a cultural change programme with full time project management teams carrying out the implementation. In manufacturing organisations, ABM was found to be a lone initiative carried out on a part time basis by staff who are not trained in project management.

All organisations however were having trouble in embedding ABM, either through inaccurate data, resource issues, or in making the connection between strategic and operational information. The findings concluded that ABM needs to be set in the strategic context of the organisation so that management and staff can understand how it contributes to the overall development of the organisation. Understanding a clearly defined purpose of the exercise is important to drive the focus of the exercise, while a successful outcome depends on management commitment, ownership, delivered benefits, and elimination of threat.

These requirements are consistent with the requirements for the implementation of any change management initiative, which begs the question as to why is there so little evidence of successful ABM? Part of the problem is in the use of the terminology. Many articles use ABC, ABM, and ABCM (Activity based Cost Management) as synonyms. I believe that there is a fundamental difference in purpose and required approach to all three applications. ABM has tended to be used to describe the approach to use the information from ABC to improve costs, and benefits have tended to be incremental. However, by linking ABM to a process perspective, and using cost and service measures, there exists a potential for achieving more significant and wide ranging benefits.

This was the approach taken by TSB, and being developed in Lloyds TSB. The benefits however have not been achieved, and so there is a desire to reassess the requirements, both in terms of the need for ABM and the key factors for successful implementation. It is intended that this research will provide a key input to this reassessment.

1.6 Identifying the Requirements: Research Objectives
There are three main objectives to the research. The first is to identify the extent to which organisations are using activity based techniques,

and specifically for process management. The coverage in the literature and at conferences has tended to focus on the experiences of organisations using ABC. Those which have wanted to extend the use of the information for other purposes such as benchmarking and improvement have found it difficult to identify similar organisations from which to learn.

The second objective is to identify the development of the techniques, in terms of the main drivers and structure of the project. Successful development of any initiative requires an understanding of the key factors which underpin the implementation and an awareness of the potential pitfalls which need to be addressed. The research will identify the key factors and constraints experienced by organisations.

The final objective is to establish if there is any link between an organisation's use of ABM for improvement purposes and the use of other process performance tools and techniques. The absence of a visible link between ABM and a defined process framework is viewed as one of the major reasons why ABM has not realised its potential within Lloyds TSB. The research will examine the relationship between the use and benefits of activity based management and the application of other process and performance tools to test this theory.

1.7 Dissertation Structure

The rise and fall of ABM in Lloyds TSB is discussed in the following chapter as a case study to provide a specific context for the need to understand the requirements. It examines the changes from the original development in TSB that took place following the merger, and assesses the impact these changes have had on the level of success in terms of implementation and benefits.

Chapter 3 reviews the literature covering process management and the provision of supporting information to identify the theory behind the requirements, and specifically the extent to which writers have discussed the link between process management and activity based information.

The research methodology is outlined in Chapter 4, and describes the reasons for undertaking the chosen approach, the development of the questionnaire, and identification of the sample population.

This is followed by two chapters that present the results and discuss the implications they provide for the implementation of successful ABM, both in general and more specifically for the development in Lloyds TSB.

The final chapter identifies the requirement for further research to build on the experience from this dissertation.

CHAPTER 2
The Development of ABM in Lloyds TSB: A Case Study

2.1 Introduction

In TSB, the development of Activity Based Management was a culmination of a four-year BPR programme and a six-year quality programme that had produced a process framework focused on the external customer. The commitment to ABM was strong and the initial outputs delivered information used by line management to identify and drive improvement to fit with the end-to-end process development carried out by the central Business Improvement team.

The merger with Lloyds was announced soon after the initial outputs were produced. Following an initial period where priority was focused on the development of the organisational infrastructure to take the business forward, ABM was relaunched. However, the benefits that have been achieved have not been as significant as those promised in the original development.

This chapter reviews the requirements behind the development, both pre- and post-merger. It examines the impact process management had on the development of ABC and ABM, and highlights the issues that have been addressed and those which remain.

2.2 Process Development in TSB

Reference to process management was first included in the TSB Strategic Plan and the five year Business Plan for the Operations Division in 1992. In an increasingly competitive environment, it was felt that the traditional approach of using ad hoc projects would not deliver the scale of change required to deliver the strategic goals of being a low cost producer, providing value for money products, with a reduced cost/income ratio. The Plans recognised the potential of a process management approach, initially to introduce process understanding and a process culture, before leading into a Business Process Reengineering (BPR) programme. The aim was to identify and develop the processes underlying *'The Vision'* to underpin the infrastructure and organisation capable of delivering competitive advantage through sustainable service improvement and cost reduction.

The key enabler for process management was the identification of an overall process model specific to TSB. This model, supported by a methodology for process improvement and redesign, was an internal adaptation and extension, in terms of both breadth and depth, of one originally created by external consultants. This to a large part enabled the best of both worlds – a proven approach to comfort the executive, but tailored to TSB's needs by a small team who knew the business and were accepted by the line.

Within the Business Plan and the methodology, integration between the core parts of the business was recognised as essential to successful process management. Cross-functional Process Owner Teams (POTs) were established to secure ownership of the identified processes and improve performance against customer service and cost standards. The resultant matrix management approach helped to open up the boundaries and stimulate the exchange of ideas, one of the first steps described by Garvin (1993) in building a learning organisation.

One of the key requirements of the POTs was to establish effective communication to the line to ensure ongoing commitment to process management. It was recognised that successful implementation of the strategy, through consistent achievement and improvement of the identified service standards, required objectives to be cascaded through the organisation, supported by defined performance measures and incentives. As the language and concepts of process became more familiar, a new culture was gradually created. Together with the development of teams responsible for complementary incremental and radical improvement, this led to a perception that a framework was being created that would allow a proactive approach to change.

As the process culture developed, there was an increasing demand for process-based measures. Information had traditionally been available and provided on a product or departmental basis, often making it difficult to compile an accurate picture of the whole, customer to customer, process where it crossed functional boundaries. To support the process perspective, information was required on a variety of dimensions to enable improved management of the key business processes through identification and prioritisation of potential improvement opportunities. External measures (reflecting performance that affects internal and external customers) and internal measures (focusing on the efficiency of the operation) were identified which reflected the critical success factors and key performance indicators emerging from the strategy.

As TSB started to further develop its process management and reengineering programme, reviews identified a number of actions to be taken forward to enable more robust management. One of these action points, building on previous work which had seen the implementation of Activity Based Costing (ABC) to provide better functional based information, was the introduction of Activity Based Management (ABM).

2.3 The Development of ABM

ABM in TSB was born out of the legacy of the ABC work and the requirements of the developing approach to process management. It was dependent on the existence of an infrastructure of process knowledge and existing measurement systems to deliver relevant cost and service information focused on the customer.

Prior to ABM, there had been a number of relatively unsuccessful attempts at applying ABC data to the process requirements. In 1993, an ABC Methodology Paper was produced which outlined the process of collecting and verifying data for the customer facing processes identified in the process model. Although the paper addressed some of the limitations of previous exercises by recognising the need for greater involvement of the main users of the output, including the POTs and the BPR Team, the focus was still on a top down allocation of costs, by a Finance team using Finance tools and techniques. The top down approach, starting with the General Ledger and allocating all costs through a set of rules, ensured financial reconciliation but created disputes at the operational level. There was a growing requirement for a more business led (i.e. not Finance) approach.

ABM was seen as a logical progression as the organisation became increasingly process oriented. The initial project proposal for ABM in 1994 stated the key objective:

'To ensure the successful alignment of management practice to activity based management to support BPM as it is rolled out...Ultimately this should lead to improvement in the service and cost performance of the Bank's processes'.

Meeting this objective would deliver benefits:

'It is by understanding our activities thoroughly that we will be in a position to continue to improve our processes in the future, to achieve competitive advantage through improved customer service and decreasing unit cost'.

For the first time there was identification of the need for both cost and service information reflecting the processes identified as critical in delivering to the customer.

By providing both cost and service information to support a variety of requirements, such as the budgeting process, customer and product profitability analysis, and in enabling identification of improvement opportunities and the implications of changing activities within a process, ABM was seen as more than an extension to ABC. It was primarily a process management tool rather than a costing tool that supported process management. This distinction is important, as most of the writing on ABM that does identify these dual purposes, such as Develin & Bellis Jones (1994) talk about ABM as being a by-product of ABC. The implications of this chicken and egg relationship are discussed in the literature review in Chapter 3.

Successful implementation of ABM required effective communication and involvement. Key stakeholders were walked through the ABM concepts; Finance and business unit representatives were co-opted onto the ABM programme. Critically, the line were continually informed of progress and showed how the information would add value in managing their business. This was a key point in overcoming the initial view of ABM information as simply replicating existing cost centre reporting, with early wins messaged to a wider audience.

ABM provided more detailed and wide ranging information within a framework created out of both local-business requirements and the organisation-wide process perspective. Information was presented in a simple form allowing identification of the linkages between activities and the whole cost of the process. This enabled understanding and management of the string of activities making up the process, at both local level through identifying and improving their part of the process, and at a business wide level in assessing the overall picture. ABM was therefore an important contributor to the objective of viewing and managing the business along process lines. The identification of activities as building blocks for processes meant that activity information could be consolidated to process information.

One of the key developments within the ABM programme, which further strengthened the process understanding, was a consistent framework for describing similar activities carried out at different sites within the Bank. The Common Activity Model (CAM) acted as a bridge between the local description of activities within a process and the generic descriptions used in the Process Model, allowing local site ownership to be retained but enabling the move to a process perspective. By providing this cross-functional perspective, the CAM enabled benchmarking of cost and service performance.

A review of the ABM programme in TSB in 1995 identified a number of critical factors required to enable success, as outlined in Table 2.1.

- A supporting process model
- The integration of process measurement information with financial information
- Multi-dimensional software and thinking
- Senior Management commitment
- Involvement of line staff to map their processes
- Facilitated by a central team to create the 'big picture' of the end-to-end processes
- An acceptance that an 80/20 approach in terms of accuracy and coverage is good enough to start

Table 2.1 Critical success factors for implementing ABM in TSB

The TSB approach to ABM was therefore significantly different to the approaches to ABM defined in textbooks or demonstrated at various conferences, and some of the differences are summarised below.

Textbook ABC/ABM/ABCM	ABM in TSB
Top down data, costs allocated by defined rules	Bottom up data, populated at activity level and consolidated by means of hierarchies
Full reconciliation of all costs to General Ledger	Focus on staff costs only, with 'sense check' reconciliation to identify reasons for discrepancies
Focus on financial data (cost and unit cost)	Focus on both cost and service information, including elapsed time and customer concerns, to provide a wider perspective of process performance
Driven by Finance function	Driven by Process Management teams

Table 2.1 Differences between textbook and TSB approaches to ABM

2.4 Redefining the Requirements: the Impact of the Merger

The merger of Lloyds and TSB at the end of 1995 provided added impetus to the previous requirements of both banks to develop a clear strategy to face the dramatic changes taking place within financial services. The need to achieve the cost benefits of the merger, the introduction of new players within the sector, and the increasing sophistication and awareness of customers required the implementation of strategies which would address external goals and deliver operational excellence. Increasingly the requirement was for the simultaneous pursuit of speed, flexibility, quality and cost efficiency, as emphasised by Harrington (1991):

"the purpose of any progressive, long lasting organisation is to provide products and services to its customers that have more value, better quality, and are less costly than other organisations offer."

The appointment in the new structure of key Senior Management staff from TSB who had been involved with the development of the process culture was an important step in enabling the redevelopment of ABM. However, the infrastructure supporting this redevelopment was different in two significant ways - the lack of a defined process model, and the driver for the delivered information.

The failure to deliver a defined process model is considered by some of the ABM practitioners within the organisation as a key factor in the 'failure' to deliver more significant benefits. Within TSB, ABM developed from a process information requirement and understanding built on a defined process framework. The new organisation is not yet at this stage, and so ABM is one of the initiatives being used to enable a process understanding and to generate the commitment to a process based approach to improvement.

Within TSB, the development of ABM was driven by the need for process based information to support the process management and redesign initiatives. It had developed almost beyond recognition from the early days when ABC data was being applied to identified processes. Within LTSB, the Group-wide ABM Project originated as part of the Group Costing Project, and was subsequently established as an independent programme under the sponsorship of the Managing Director, Central Operations, with executive sponsorship from the Deputy Chief Executive. Strong links remained with the Costing Project, with the intention of using the ABM data to enhance the top-level costs generated by the Costing Project.

However, to ensure a focus remained on the process aspects, the Group-wide ABM team established to implement the project reiterated the identified benefits proposed in the TSB project proposal, that the information would lead to *'more effective management of activities and processes and enable cost reduction and service improvements. ABM supports both Continuous Improvement and Business Process Reengineering.'* Critically, it was recognised that coherence would only come from the adoption of a common process framework. The one sentence definition outlined the role of the Group-wide ABM team:

"*To develop, implement and support the management of end to end processes in terms of cost and service in order that improvement can be achieved and maintained.*"

Although the project was Group-wide, it was recognised that

29

implementation would have to be phased according to business needs, with various initiatives of different scope coordinated under the common framework. Local involvement and ownership was seen as critical to the success of the project, and so it was agreed that business units would generate, maintain and use the information, enabled by the provision of tools, techniques and a common framework and methodology provided by the central team. However, as the responsibility for defining processes was pushed further down the structure, the original *raison d'etre* of the ABM approach was, for many people, being lost. The full end-to-end, customer-to-customer, perspective was being fragmented into smaller pictures.

Increasingly, the ABM information was being seen as a replication of information provided by other measurement systems that had been established to enable control and improvement. Its role as a provider of process measurement, to enable the process manager to identify the extent to which the process is meeting expectations and to highlight the results of change, was being lost.

The fact that ABM has not been embraced within Lloyds TSB to the same extent that seemed likely in TSB masks the belief among the people involved in progressing ABM that the Lloyds TSB approach is significantly ahead of other companies. Attendance at seminars and conferences suggest that the label of ABM is often interchangeable with ABC, or at best recognised that the cost information should be used to aid decision making in terms of customer or product profitability. The link to processes and the use of the information to identify and develop improvement opportunities covering both cost and service is rarely mentioned.

2.5 Issues of Implementation
The pitfalls identified by Player & Keys (1995) had been addressed in the TSB implementation, and this was reflected in the belief that ABM would deliver significant cost and service benefits. However, the major organisational changes and immediate priorities that resulted from the merger with Lloyds meant that the momentum was halted. The re-launch in the new organisation, with a change in supporting background and scope, has meant that not all of the issues have been

dealt with to the same extent as previously. Although the theory is stronger, putting it into practice has been more difficult.

Within Lloyds TSB it has been difficult to identify significant benefits from the work that has been carried out to date. The ABM framework has in part been used by Finance to provide a more robust ABC model, but so far has not been used to achieve its initial objectives of delivering significant process improvements. After five years of stop/start progress, there is a widespread feeling that something more should have been achieved. With the development of other, more localised, performance measurement systems, and a focus on the latest quality initiatives and models, there is a danger that the commitment to further develop and maintain ABM may be curtailed.

So, is the Lloyds TSB approach to ABM more developed than other companies, and if so, why has it failed to deliver what it should have delivered? In TSB there was a move, which was never fulfilled, to develop a process based organisation. The functional development, responsibilities, and targets within Lloyds TSB have led to some resistance to the package behind a process perspective. It may be that this is the biggest barrier to achieving radical benefits.

2.6 Objectives of the Research for Lloyds TSB

Within Lloyds TSB, the approach to ABM is being reassessed in the light of other initiatives. Although there has been significant work in developing a methodology and identifying the dependent links to other tools, the support and commitment required to address the potential pitfalls documented by Player & Keys (1995) and summarised in Appendix 3, is not as visible as in the TSB development.

From a business point of view, the objective of my work, through reviewing the literature and carrying out the survey, will be to benchmark the Lloyds TSB approach against both published theory and identified practice. This will confirm, or otherwise, the belief that the framework exists to enable significant benefits through better understanding of activities and processes. The work will also identify the extra requirements to fully exploit the potential of ABM.

CHAPTER 3
The Requirements for Process and Activity Management: A Review of Published Material

3.1 Introduction

This chapter presents a description and critical analysis of writings on process management and the use of activity information. It addresses separately the literature covering the two approaches before considering the extent to which they have been linked.

This review, as well as providing an input to defining the purpose of ABM and the factors which enable successful implementation, identifies the gaps in current understanding and so guides the research requirements and approach.

3.2 Process Literature

Throughout the 1980s there was a growing interest in understanding and managing business processes as companies tried to seek new ways to face the increasingly competitive environment created by an expanding global market and technical innovation. The Massachusetts Institute of Technology (MIT) carried out extensive studies between 1984 and 1989 into the management methods most likely to contribute to success over the following decade (the 'Management in the 1990s' programme). One of the findings highlighted the use of information technology to facilitate ways of streamlining processes, and this was followed up and elaborated on by a number of authors.

There is now a wealth of published material, supported by an increasing number of conferences and seminars, highlighting the need for cross-functional process management to enable effective delivery of an organisation's strategic objectives. The two main themes have been the need for process understanding across the organisation, and the need for supporting holistic performance measures.

Understanding and documenting the key cross-functional processes are critical steps in business process management, without which it is difficult to move on to process improvement (Harrington 1995).

Much of the original focus was on Business Process Re-engineering (BPR), and most notable in terms of promoting awareness and debate of BPR was an article in the Harvard Business Review by an MIT professor (Hammer 1990). This outlined the concept of process re-engineering as the key method to enable dramatic improvements in the critical measures of performance. These ideas were given a wider audience with the publication of a book that provided the rationale for thinking and acting process (Hammer & Champy 1993).

Although this focus on BPR generated a tidal wave of interest in process management, there has since been widespread criticism as well as support, which has had an impact on the extent to which it has been integrated as a key factor in an organisation's behaviour. Writers such as Harrington (1998) have targeted their criticism at the anticipated benefits of the re-engineering approach rather than the principle of developing and acting on a process framework. However, this 'failure' has contributed to the slowdown in the scope of implementation by many organisations in terms of a clearly defined and communicated process model or framework.

Many organisations have used the BPM label without understanding its true application in terms of cross-functional management (Zairi 1997). BPM is an approach dependent on many factors combining to deliver customer requirements in an optimum and satisfactory way. Zairi proposes a set of rules to assist in the development of a BPM culture, including the management of processes through various performance improvement measurement and targets. In this context, ABM can be seen as an integral tool to support process management. This moves away from a focus on the information itself to how the information is used.

The effective delivery of strategic objectives requires a framework supported by process orientated management, currently beyond the reach of most companies which tend to govern by functional cost targets (Lee & Dale 1998). The failure to continue to progress and develop the TSB process model into the new organisation, as outlined in chapter 2, has had an impact on the level of process understanding and management. This in turn is also seen as a contributory factor to the failure of the ABM programme to deliver more significant benefits.

The extent to which a process model influences the actions of other organisations is addressed in my research.

Cross-functional process management requires information that can describe and monitor the business processes and encourage learning and understanding (Garvin 1993). A research paper looking at accelerating performance improvements in business processes supports this view. Survey results showed anticipation of significant future process improvements through the development of integrative, open information systems (Smeds 1996). Management information must enable improvements to business processes, and as they consist of a series of linked activities that deliver products and services to customers, the information must reflect the customer's perspective and provide the visibility to enable understanding and action to drive towards delivery of the overall strategic objectives (Develin & Bellis-Jones 1995).

Activity based information provides the basis for much of this need, although its capability to drive process change has not been widely exploited. Its origins were founded out of the limitations of conventional costing information, and only recently has the potential to extend its influence to process management been highlighted.

3.3 Development of Activity Based Techniques
The theory behind activity based approaches to management information started with activity based costing (ABC), which acquired prominence in the late 1980s following work by Johnson and Kaplan (1987). Their book, *'Relevance Lost: the Rise and Fall of Management Accounting'* dealt with findings from a number of case studies which highlighted the inadequacies of conventional costing and cost management techniques in meeting the requirements of a new and changing competitive environment with a proliferation of products, services, and customers. This work opened up a debate on the issue of management information, and in particular the increasing demand to provide accurate measurement of the cost of resources used to design and produce products and sell and deliver them to customers.

The identification of activities and cost drivers as a foundation for improved analysis and understanding of an organisation's costs was a key factor in delivering this measurement (Cooper & Kaplan 1991). The development of an activity based perspective enabled identification of the variable costs of using resources rather than the fixed costs of supplying them. This allowed improved understanding of the true cost of developing products and delivering to customers. The key message was to use this understanding to improve profits through a combination of reducing the number of activities and increasing the efficiency of performing the remainder.

Cooper and Kaplan have been at the forefront of research into the experience of implementing activity based techniques. Much of their initial work is summarised in *The Design of Cost Management Systems* (Cooper & Kaplan 1991), which describes the benefits gained by companies that had moved from traditional cost accounting to an activity based approach. This work generated increased interest, and a host of books, articles and seminars from companies and consultants who could describe their experiences in implementing ABC became available. However, the experiences described were mainly those of companies who believed they had successfully implemented ABC, and usually targeted at management accountants. The link to the parallel development of process management theory was not being made.

Although Porter (1985) discusses activities from a strategic point of view, introducing the value chain as a basic tool for a systematic examination of all activities performed by an organisation, it is only in recent years that the potential for extending ABC has been considered. Many authors, such as Plowman (1997), Lambert and Whitworth (1996), touch on the potential of activity based costing techniques to provide a foundation on which to build solutions to many of the critical business issues facing organisations.

This potential to use the information for all aspects of management, moving away from the original emphasis on product costing, is taking up by Develin & Bellis-Jones (1995). Critically, they identify the need for a level of accuracy that enables managers to take informed tactical and strategic decisions, something which conventional financial and management control systems do not provide. Their use of the term Activity Based Cost Management (ABCM) describes this widening of the original scope and its attachment to a particular management style and philosophy. Again though, the emphasis is on improvement being driven by costs with limited reference to the impact on cross functional processes and the required framework to exploit the potential of using the information.

One of the few references to the requirement for a framework is by Greenwood & Reeve (1992). They outline the potential of extending ABC models, originally designed to support strategic decision making about products and customers, to the support of operational decision making. They believe that although many articles alluded to the potential of using activity based information to foster process oriented improvements, there is an apparent void in the literature of a comprehensive methodology designed to relate cost and performance information to processes at the activity level.

Part of this problem is that activity based techniques are still seen very much as part of the Management Accountants toolbag, placing the emphasis on the financial aspects of the information. To achieve the full management potential of ABC, there must be a conscious process of organisational change and implementation (Cooper 1996). It needs to be viewed as a management system rather than a financial system, owned by the functions and designed to management requirements, not financial accounting.

In moving to the use of the information for improvement, there is a recognition that more people in the organisation must become involved to focus on the issues and identify supporting information requirements (Kaplan 1995; Cooper 1996). If the information requirements are driven solely by the accountant, it may not be as relevant as it should be in addressing the key operational issues. This requires the management accountant to become more involved with the operational line rather than be seen mainly as part of the finance function. Supporting this view, Kershaw & Mahenthiran (1998) report on a study by the Institute of Management Accountants on their changing role to one of business partners becoming more involved in strategic planning, performance evaluation and business process management.

The increasing emphasis on the management of activities has brought about new terminology and acronyms that has led to similar confusion and concerns as to the variations used in process management. ABC is concerned with costs. It is a technical costing theory designed to stimulate management action (Argyris & Kaplan 1994); a provider of more accurate cost information about business activities and processes, and of the products, services and customers served by these processes (Kaplan 1996). However, ABC information is only useful to the extent that it is used to manage better and should be viewed as a planning tool rather than a tool for examining how well or poorly managers or organisational units performed in the past (Cokins 1996).

In recent years there has been increasing use of ABCM and ABM to highlight the extent to which ABC information can be used, in enabling decisions about activities, products, customers, and other cost objects (Player & Keys 1995). Hixon (1995) defines ABM as the management and control of enterprise performance using activity based information as the primary means of decision support. Compendiums of articles have been published (e.g. Brinker 1993) which link the delivery of cost information to its application as a decision support tool. Brimson (1994) argues that ABM provides the tools and information needed to support managers in attaining enterprise excellence, enabling better decisions and a change in company culture. Again though, the emphasis is on the management of cost information, which suggests that ABC drives ABM. As the TSB experience shows, this does not have to be the case, and it may be better to integrate the approaches after fully understanding the information requirements.

The discussions on activity based approaches vary between the cost management writers and the process writers, mainly in respect of the perspectives used and the objectives of the analysis. Cost management writers follow the Kaplan, Cooper, and Johnson emphasis on costing and cost management, with the objective of focusing on how activities are performed and why they occur and consume resources in the manner they do. Process writers such as Porter (1985) and Harrington (1991) discuss activities from a strategic perspective. The focus is the process, not the activities as such, with the objective of the activity analysis being process improvement. This view is supported by a recent KPMG study that assesses the impact of process based management on seven leading UK companies. A key factor is the provision of information on the cost, quality and outputs of an activity chain as a basis for continuous process improvement.

Zairi (1997) in trying to explain BPM, outlines a number of rules that govern the approach, including a focus on the customer through the linking of activities, supported by the provision of meaningful and visible measurement - rules that are shared by ABM. As the parallel strands of activity and process, information and management seem to be logically linked, it is surprising that the links have not been more clearly or widely promoted.

3.4 Linking Activity to Process Management

Effective management of change requires the management of cross functional business processes (Hammer & Champy 1993), which in turn requires relevant information to describe and monitor performance. As processes consist of a series of linked activities that deliver products and services to customers, activity based information specifically meets this requirement (Develin & Bellis-Jones 1995). Its objective is to provide the information needed to improve business processes, and then sustain the improvement fundamental to long-term survival (Miller 1992). By providing financial and operating information to reflect the performance of activities, ABM has in place a system to monitor continuous improvement and manage the business from a process perspective rather than a departmental one (Borjesson 1994). The proviso is that actions need to be taken as a result of the information.

Activity based techniques have been linked to other management tools and techniques. Letza and Gadd (1994) consider the use of ABC to support Total Quality Management, arguing that as ABC considers the use of resources consumed by activities according to processes, it offers TQM an accurate management information system that will provide cost data at the business process level.

3.5 Issues of Implementation

If activity based management is considered as an enabler to support process management, it can be assumed that the requirements for successful implementation are common. Although there are many articles outlining the problems facing the implementation of change management initiatives, little has been written specifically on why ABM projects fall short of their intended goals. However, that which has supports the view that ABM and BPM share common problems.

This is notable in the series of three articles by Player & Keys (1995) examining the ten pitfalls that can occur in each part of the three-prong implementation of ABM - getting off to the right start; developing the pilot; and moving from pilot to mainstream. The articles cover both behavioural and technical issues arising from interviews with 50 people who were either implementing ABM, using ABM information, ABM consultants, or managers who had rejected ABM. Any of the pitfalls can cause ABM to fail, but if they are recognised and dealt with there is more chance of success. These pitfalls are outlined in Appendix 3, and can be viewed as a summary of the growing number of articles highlighting the requirements and problems of implementing any new initiative. However, the pitfalls identified by Player & Keys were addressed in the implementation of ABM in TSB but problems still existed. This suggests that the requirements for successful implementation are not simply the flipside of the pitfalls.

Several writers (Player & Keys 1995, Cokins 1996, Cooper 1996) have identified the requirements for successful implementation of activity based techniques, although mainly for costing purposes rather than holistic process management. However, it has been argued that the implementation of any change management initiative faces similar issues, only differentiated by the extent of the impact.

Argyris & Kaplan (1994) use the development and implementation of ABC as an example to outline the requirements for the implementation of any new technical theory in an organisation. They state the necessary pre-conditions of internal consistency and external validity need to be met before addressing the three main requirements of education, sponsorship, and internal commitment. This commitment requires managers to recognise the usefulness of ABC for decision-making purposes. However, end users often see it as more financial information that does not supply their need for business driven information.

Building on these requirements, Develin & Bellis-Jones (1995) identify the further key requirements of clarity of purpose and ownership as critical to the implementation of ABM. It can only be successfully applied if it is shown as a means of achieving the defined and communicated objectives of the organisation. The implementation of an ABM programme needs to be linked to the strategy and the required integrated approach to change can only be pulled together at the top. This involves setting direction and defining the process vision at the top level, and then initiating an integrated programme that introduces a new management culture, within an overall framework, that motivates people at all levels in the organisation to flesh out the strategy and make it work. If any process related initiative is to succeed, appropriate goals need to be established and communicated.

These requirements were reiterated at a conference organised by CIMA in May 1995, where the critical success factors for ABM were developed - senior management commitment; ownership; clarity of purpose; and credibility (in terms of the information produced). Although organised by a body of management accountants, the conference stresses that ABM is a MIS tool rather than an accounting tool.

Borjesson (1994) argues that it is important to have a clear objective in order to gather the appropriate type of activity information and therefore exploit the potential improvement opportunities. Both quantitative information for costing purposes and qualitative information for activity control is required, each serving different purposes. The quantitative approach, to identify what activities are performed and their resource requirements, is sufficient when activity information is used for costing purposes. However, activity information to enable management action requires further attributes, such as links and interdependencies between activities, cycle times, identification of value and non-value activities.

Case studies show that there is a need to clearly define the purpose of the relevant activity based approach and for measurement to match the purpose. Too many activity based projects have been initiated with only vague insights about the impact of implementation (Player & Keys 1995).

The original focus of ABC was on the manufacturing sector. Antos (1992) argues that implementing the techniques in service organisations is more difficult as they are less homogeneous than in the manufacturing sector. Manufacturers perform many of the same type of activities in similar ways, but he considers that there is little similarity between different activities in service organisations. This is something that was considered in TSB with the development of a Common Activity Model that served to identify fundamentally similar activities by considering their purpose.

One of the main reasons behind this failure is the independent approach taken to various management initiatives. A review of the literature covering process management by Lee & Dale (1998) concludes that there is a need to integrate the use of a variety of improvement tools such as re-engineering, continuous improvement and benchmarking. A similar point is made by Hoffman (1997) who says that instead of focusing on one particular improvement strategy at the exclusion of others, use should be made of a variety of approaches, tools and techniques for improving products, systems and processes.

3.6 Research Context

The research attempts to build on this discussion of the literature. There is clearly a need to gain further understanding of the purpose of the various activity based techniques and the extent to which they are being used to enable business improvement. The focus of the literature covered in this chapter is on the theory of process management and activity information, as separate entities. There has been limited writing on the practical application and need to manage activities within a process context through the delivery of cost and service information. The research and this dissertation attempt to fill some of the gaps in the understanding of these aspects.

The research examines the factors considered by organisations with experience of implementing activity based information as critical to success, as well as the constraints that need to be addressed. This will help to identify the extent to which organisations have the required theoretical background and understanding of the common principles required for the implementation of any management initiative.

CHAPTER 4
Collecting Experiences of ABM: Research Methodology

4.1 Introduction

This chapter identifies the requirements for, and the approach taken, to obtain new information to support and extend the literature surrounding the knowledge of ABM. The rationale governing the research strategy and objectives is followed by an explanation of the development of the questionnaire and the selection of the target population. An overview of the survey and analysis process completes the account of the methodology.

4.2 The Need for Research on ABM

Reviewing the literature on the development, implementation and use of activity based techniques, it became clear that there was inconsistency in the terminology used and in their application. The potential for building on the basic activity cost information has been identified by an increasing number of writers, such as Develin & Bellis-Jones (1995), Greenwood & Reeve (1992). However, as the theoretical link to process management becomes more widely recognised, documented case studies and the understanding of practical requirements become less prevalent.

Previous surveys on the extent to which activity based techniques are used in organisations have been mainly American based, often carried out by consultancies or management forums, and have produced inconclusive findings in terms of the benefits of implementation. This is often seen to be a result of the confusion that surrounds the terminology, objectives or approaches of the various techniques. Without a common understanding, it is difficult to build on the potential that exists to deliver the specific requirements of an organisation.

The development of ABM, originally across TSB and now in parts of Lloyds TSB, had led to an approach considered (admittedly by the internal project team) to be significantly ahead of other companies and methodologies espoused by management consultants. Attendance at seminars and conferences suggested that the label of ABM was being used in a much more limited way than it was in TSB or in which it was developing in Lloyds TSB. In particular, the link to end-to-end processes and the use of holistic performance information to identify and develop improvement opportunities covering both cost and service was rarely mentioned, let alone experienced.

However, although benefits have been identified, there is a widespread feeling that after five years of (admittedly stop/start) progress, more should have been achieved. The move away from a clearly defined process framework, the development of other, more localised, performance measurement systems, and a focus on the latest quality initiatives and models, has led to a review of the requirements for and of ABM. To support this review, there is a need to reassess the purpose and approach, and to understand the requirements for ABM to be used as an improvement tool, in particular to identify if its use in this way is dependent on a process culture.

4.3 Research Strategy and Objectives

The main objective of the research is to identify the key factors that enable successful implementation of ABM. There was a belief coming out of the TSB approach that, of the many enabling requirements, the most significant factor was the link to a process framework that reflected the organisation's objectives. Experience had also shown, supported by the literature (e.g. Player & Keys 1995), that there were many other behavioural and technical issues to consider. I wanted to gain an understanding of the requirements so that I could test whether an infrastructure had been established in Lloyds TSB to enable successful implementation.

The review of the development of ABM in TSB and Lloyds TSB, discussed in Chapter 2, provided a benchmark case study against which I could compare practical experiences of other organisations and key theory from the literature. To enable the collection of a significant amount of standard data, suitable for comparison, from a sizeable population, a questionnaire-based survey was chosen as the main research method. As well as meeting the above criteria, the time factor was also an important influence and the questionnaire would allow the collection of a significant amount of data over a relatively short period, with minimal imposition on the identified respondents.

The main drawback of the questionnaire approach, apart from the capacity to do it badly, is that the data collected may not be as wide ranging as that collected by other qualitative research methods (Saunders, Lewis & Thornhill 1997). This issue would in part be addressed by supplementing the questionnaire results with more detailed qualitative information gained from interviews carried out with a sample of the respondents.

This approach would deliver a clearer understanding of the extent to which organisations are using activity based techniques; the purpose for which they are being used; the approach to implementation of the techniques; and finally to identify the influence of other initiatives on the use of the techniques. Obtaining a common practical understanding of what has previously been a theoretical concept would enable a wider and more consistent discussion of approaches and best practice. From a Lloyds TSB perspective, a reassessment of the approach used, together with the findings from the survey, would also provide input to the future development of the ABM programme.

4.4 The Survey

The survey needed to provide a significant amount of information to add to the understanding gained from the literature of the requirements for, and the use of, activity based techniques. Specifically it needed to address the gaps in relation to the understanding of the practical application of activity based information for process management and improvement.

Reliable and valid results were dependent on a robust, wide ranging questionnaire being completed by as large a sample as possible. The approach taken to address these requirements, in terms of the development of the questionnaire and the selection of the sample population, as well as the process of carrying out the survey and analysing the results, are outlined below.

4.4.1 The questionnaire

The questionnaire addresses the three main research objectives - to identify the extent to which organisations are using activity based techniques; to identify the development of activity based techniques within organisations; and to establish the background of organisations undertaking activity based techniques in terms of the use of other process and performance tools.

The questions were influenced by personal experience within Lloyds TSB, a review of the literature, and by the limitations of previous surveys. They needed to elicit responses that would provide three different levels of output: a descriptive understanding of the various acronyms in use; an identification of the different approaches and their impact on the application and use; and an understanding of the requirements to enable activity based information to be used as a tool to deliver, or support the delivery of, business process improvements.

The questionnaire would identify the extent to which organisations have acknowledged potential barriers in the approaches used. Analysis would contribute to the discussion of best practice for implementing ABM as an integral tool of process management. The starting point however was to gain an understanding of the terminology and purpose behind the implementation of activity based techniques.

The related, often interchangeable, acronyms in use throughout the literature and in practice lead to confusion and a reduced opportunity to learn from best practice. ABC, ABM, ABCM, ABB, provide different emphases for different writers and organisations. A consistent approach to any new initiative requires a clearly defined and shared understanding of the requirements and expected outcomes. An activity framework to be used for improving the efficiency and effectiveness of an organisation is likely to require different levels of detail from one focused on costing. The first section of the questionnaire approaches these issues and the scope of the implementation.

The second section deals with the approaches to implementation, an area which has produced a significant amount of literature, both directly related to activity based techniques and change management initiatives in general. The questions were based on the main factors identified through the literature and at an ABM conference organised by CIMA in 1995 as critical to successful implementation. These included the level of senior management commitment, ownership, clarity of purpose, and the extent of active and visible support.

The third section allows examination of the suggested theory that the organisational background, in terms of the application of other process, performance or quality tools and techniques, has an influence on the development and use of the activity based techniques. This is an area that has not been covered in depth in the literature, but has been considered as a key factor in the belief that the TSB approach, in terms of depth and scope, was significantly ahead of others in its potential.

For each of the sections, a number of questions were generated and then reviewed with colleagues to determine the most appropriate ones in terms of meeting the objectives and enabling relevant analysis, and to ensure that they were clear and consistent for the respondents. Previous questionnaires and research textbooks were reviewed to ensure that the design was as welcoming and user friendly as possible. Other components identified by Saunders, Lewis and Thornhill as essential to increasing the level of response were also developed. These included a promise of confidentiality and a statement that anonymous replies would be accepted; the provision of contact numbers; and an explanatory covering letter outlining the purpose of the research and a willingness to share the results.

4.4.2 The participants

Fifty questionnaires were issued to nominated individuals in three types of organisation: those who had expressed an interest in ABM; those who had won the UK Quality Award and therefore could be assumed to have an integral process framework; and TSB/Lloyds TSB. (These categories are not necessarily mutually exclusive, and in fact questionnaires were sent to different parts of BT under the guise of both ABM and Quality).

These individuals were selected as there was a strong likelihood, because of their background, that they would understand the objectives and welcome involvement in the research. The fact that the questionnaires were sent to individuals who had pronounced an interest in ABM, and to identified contacts in organisations having a successful Quality philosophy, led to an expectation that a response rate could be achieved which was significantly higher than a generally acceptable figure of 30%. The limitations of the research as a result of the specific approach taken in the selection of the sample population are discussed in Chapter 7.

Forty questionnaires were issued to individuals included in the Activity Based Management Contacts Register issued by the Employers' Group of the Chartered Institute of Management Accountants (CIMA). The Register was set up in response to requests from members of the Employers' Group and others for a way to make contact with individuals who had experience of, or who were considering implementing, activity based techniques. This complemented the ABM Exchange events initiated in 1995 by the North East England Regional Employers' Group and facilitated by a team of practitioners from the University of Northumbria and the University of Teesside. Their aim was to discuss practical issues arising from companies' first hand experiences, and to pool and exchange ideas to enable identification of best practice.

Eight questionnaires were issued to organisations that had won the UK Quality Award for Business Excellence in the past five years. Individuals in these organisations were identified following a request to the British Quality Foundation. Information from this group would help to identify the extent to which organisations considered as having an integral process framework used activity based techniques to support process management.

As a benchmark, I arranged for the Project Manager responsible for developing ABM in TSB to complete a questionnaire from the perspective of the situation in 1995, immediately prior to the merger. The set was completed by the Project Manager responsible for coordinating ABM within Lloyds TSB, who provided an up to date perspective.

4.4.3 The process
The self-administered questionnaires, supported by an accompanying

letter outlining the purpose of the survey *(Appendix 1)* and a stamped addressed envelope for the reply, were posted on Monday 2nd November, with returns requested by Wednesday 18th November. A follow up letter was faxed to the 23 individuals who had not replied by the 18th, which brought a further six replies. Responses were input to a Lotus 1-2-3 spreadsheet as they were returned.

Five respondents who had indicated a willingness to discuss their replies were telephoned to obtain further information on their experiences of evaluating and implementing their particular activity based techniques. To support one of the main objectives of the research, the selection of these interviewees was biased towards those respondents who had identified an interest in the use of the information for improvement purposes.

4.4.4 The analysis

After a review of proprietary database applications available at work, I chose to use the simple, effective, (and available at home) Lotus 1-2-3 software. The design of the questionnaire enabled simple coding of responses, and once these were input the initial high level quantitative results were easily obtained. Further detailed analysis of the responses in terms of dependencies was effected by the database query tools available in 1-2-3. As well as the basic analysis of all the returns to address the research objectives, work was also carried out to identify differences in approach, expectations and backgrounds between the CIMA- and Quality-sourced organisations, and to compare with the approach undertaken in Lloyds TSB. Although the approach to the analysis was largely based on an understanding of the need to address the issues identified both in the literature and from the experience of Lloyds TSB, it also followed the guidelines discussed in Saunders, Lewis and Thornhill (1997).

Of the 50 questionnaires issued, 34 found their way back (68%). However, two of these were from management consultants who advise clients on how to implement ABM rather than use it within their organisations. They therefore did not complete the questionnaire, although a follow up interview with one of the consultants did generate some informative comments. These will be outlined in Chapter 6 as part of the discussion into the overall findings of the survey. One other questionnaire was returned uncompleted, with a covering letter simply stating that the organisation did not use ABM. Unlike other returns, there was no information included in section 3 of the questionnaire, which was aimed at all respondents regardless of their position in terms of ABM. Analysis was therefore carried out on the responses from 31 questionnaires.

The development of the questionnaire focused on the means to meet the research objectives. Identifying the extent to which organisations are using activity based techniques, the approaches to the development of those techniques, and the influence of other management tools and models on their implementation and use would hopefully provide new information and understanding. The extent to which this has happened is presented in the following two chapters covering the detailed results and conclusions.

CHAPTER 5
Presentation of the Evidence: Research Findings

5.1 Introduction
This chapter presents the results from the questionnaire and forms the basis for the discussion provided in the following chapter. As well as the quantitative data, comments made by the participants, either on the questionnaire or during the follow-up discussions, are also included.

The results are presented in sections that reflect each part of the questionnaire, which in turn were developed to address the research objectives. The following three sections relate to the individual parts of the questionnaire: the extent to which organisations are using activity based techniques; the development of activity based techniques; and organisation background. More detailed analysis using criteria from each part of the questionnaire is provided in section 5.5. The key findings from this analysis will be the main focus of the discussion in the following chapter.

Of the 50 questionnaires issued, 31 were returned completed and form the base for these findings. Two of the questionnaires were returned anonymously, but of those that included details of their organisation 33% were from manufacturing; 23% from financial services; 17% from both retail and public sectors, and 10% from other service industries. However, as there was not a significant difference in the results from these groupings, no analysis by sector has been included in this chapter.

A simple presentation of the base data, giving the number and percentage of responses to the choices for each question, is provided in Appendix 2.

5.2 The Use of Activity Based Techniques
The first part of the questionnaire seeks to identify the extent to which organisations are using activity based techniques, and addresses description, coverage, purpose, and the type of benefits achieved or anticipated.

The composition of the sample, in terms of the use of activity based information, is shown in Figure 5.1. The four respondents who stated that their organisations were not considering using activity based information all believed that they would do so in the future.

Fig. 5.1 Composition of the sample in terms of the use of activity based information

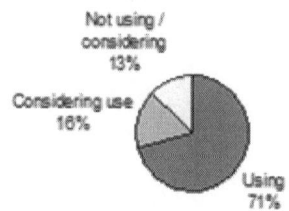

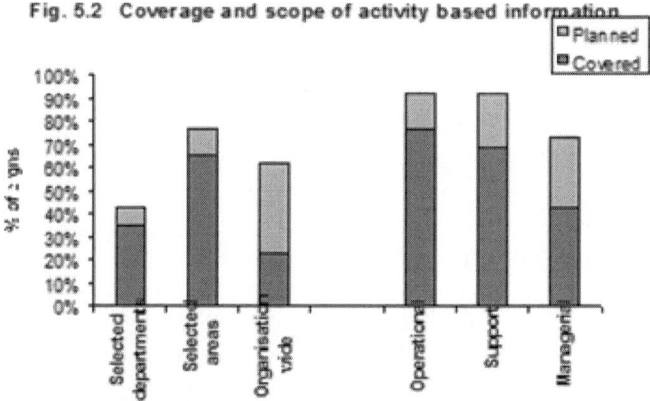

Fig. 5.2 Coverage and scope of activity based information

In the organisations where activity based information has been or is about to be implemented, the emphasis in terms of the scope of coverage is on its application in selected departments or functions rather than across the whole organisation. The focus of the information is on operational and support activities, already covered by over 70% of cases, and expected to be covered by 92%. Managerial activities have also been included by 42% of the organisations, with a further 31% planning to do so. These findings are shown in Figure 5.2.

One of the problems in understanding the requirements for successful application of any activity based information and management is the terminology used to describe the various techniques. As shown in the literature review, although there are benefits in providing discrete definitions, the various acronyms are often interchanged within the same article. This makes it difficult to identify the appropriate technique for the required purpose, and to gain experience of best practice.

Activity Based Costing (ABC) was the preferred choice in this research, with 81% of respondents saying that it was used in their organisation. In one-third of the sample, it was the only term used. Activity Based Management (ABM) was used by 42%, although mainly in conjunction with ABC – only three of the 31 organisations used it on its own. Of the organisations using the term ABM, only one-third had a definition of what it entails, each one including reference to the extension of ABC data to enable decisions or to identify and drive business improvement opportunities.

One of the objectives of the research was to identify the purpose and benefits of using activity based information. The requirement for relevant financial information was found to be the main driver, with two-thirds of the organisations identifying the provision of more accurate information on the cost and profitability of products and customers as the main purpose. The provision of relevant information to enable process improvement activity was identified as best describing the purpose by 19%, with the remaining 15% indicating equal importance to the two requirements.

This emphasis on the financial aspects was reiterated in the benefits identified from the use of activity based information. A number of potential benefits were provided, ranging from more accurate application of costs through to improved customer service. The respondents were asked to indicate which of the benefits had been achieved, or were expected to be achieved, in their organisation as a result of using this information. Figure 5.3 below shows the findings.

Fig. 5.3 Benefits identified from using activity based information

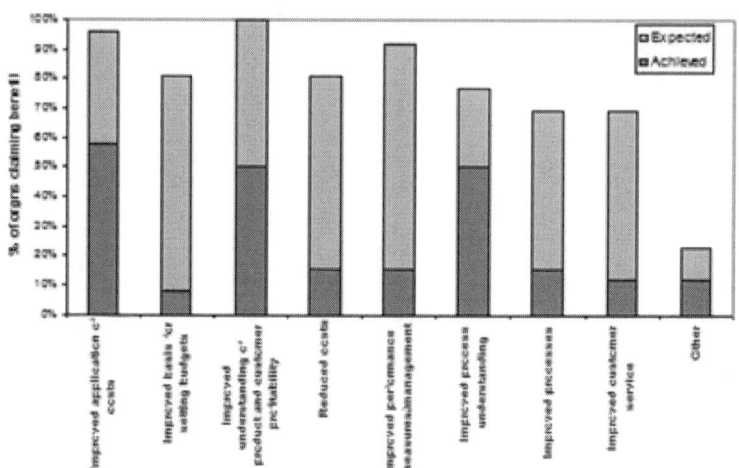

Benefits had been achieved by 86% of the organisations that had developed activity based information. More accurate application of costs, leading to improved understanding of product and customer profitability were the main benefits, together with improved process understanding. These had been all been achieved in over 40% of the cases. However, for the other potential benefits outlined, there was a significant gap between expectation and achievement. This was particularly noticeable for the hard benefits of reduced costs, improved processes and improved customer service.

The 'other benefits' identified related to the provision of information for strategic purposes, improved ownership and responsibility for performance data, and as a catalyst for other improvement initiatives.

5.3 The Development of Activity Based Techniques
The second part of the questionnaire was concerned with the drivers for the activity based techniques and the support provided for implementation.

Again, the financial aspects were dominant in terms of the decisions to implement the techniques. The Finance Director or equivalent was identified as the main driver behind the development by 90% of respondents. Reflecting this, a requirement for improved financial information was identified as an influence on the decision to use or investigate the use of activity based techniques by 92% of the respondents. This was followed by a requirement to support process understanding (62%) and strategic business objectives (54%). There was limited acknowledgement of the influence of information from published material, conferences, or consultants on the decision to consider the techniques.

Although just over half of the organisations identified strategic business objectives as influencing the decision to use activity based information, once it was implemented over 80% indicated that they had established a link between the objectives and the information.

A Project Team was set up by 90% of the organisations to drive forward implementation. Again, Finance staff played a dominant role, mainly in conjunction with Operations staff. Staff from areas responsible for change management were included on less than a third of the teams, although slightly more used external consultants. All of the teams used a formal project plan, mostly developed internally, although this was also identified as one of the roles of the external consultants in 20% of the cases. Steering Committees, used in 40% of the implementations, drew staff in similar proportions.

Although identified as a separate project, only 38% of the organisations had established a budget to support development and implementation. Interestingly, those that had done so were twice as likely to identify cost as being one of the constraints to which the project was subjected. All the respondents identified one or more constraints to development and implementation. Resource was the main issue, although with the exception of technology, identified by 40% of the respondents, all of the other declared constraints were identified as a factor in over half of the implementations. These are shown in Figure 5.4.

The development of activity based information required both existing and new data to support activities which were identified mainly from a bottom up basis, although in half of the cases this was supplemented by reference to a top down approach.

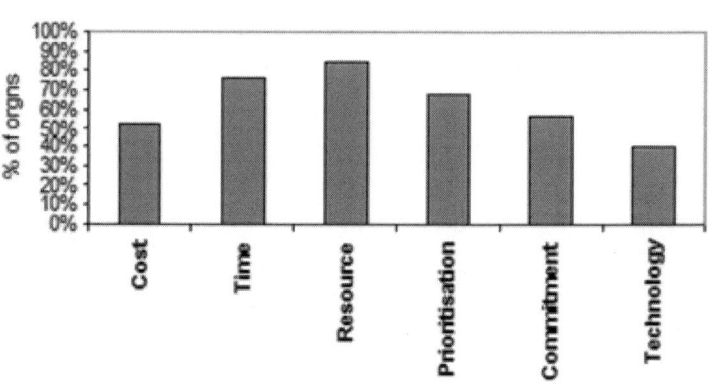

Fig. 5.4 Factors constraining implementation of activity based information

A variety of software tools were used for analysis, ranging from standard spreadsheet applications, through to off-the-shelf and bespoke packages. The most common single application mentioned was HyperABC although most organisations had developed applications internally. Only one reply included a process mapping tool that was used to communicate process cost information.

5.4 Organisational Background

The final part of the questionnaire was developed to gain an understanding of the influence that other aspects of an organisation has on the development and use of activity based techniques and information. It addresses the use of other tools and approaches to management, and these criteria will be overlayed on the results from the other parts of the questionnaire and shown in the following section. This part was aimed at all respondents, irrespective of their involvement with any form of activity based information, and so the percentages, unless stated otherwise relate to the 31 replies received.

84% of the organisations had implemented other recognised

management and information tools or systems, with Continuous Improvement and TQM being the most common. 77% of the organisations had established training programmes to support some of the identified initiatives. These findings are summarised in Figure 5.5.

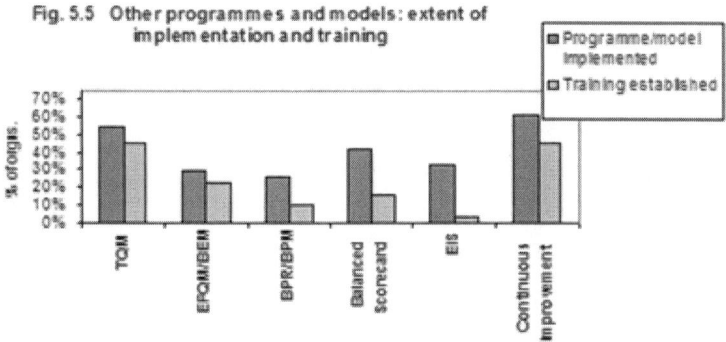

One of the key objectives of the research was to identify the influence of a process improvement background on the development and use of activity based techniques. Figure 5.6 indicates the extent to which process and performance management is established within the sample organisations, and these criteria will be used to further analyse the findings from the first part of the questionnaire in terms of the purpose and benefits of activity based information. These findings are shown in the following section.

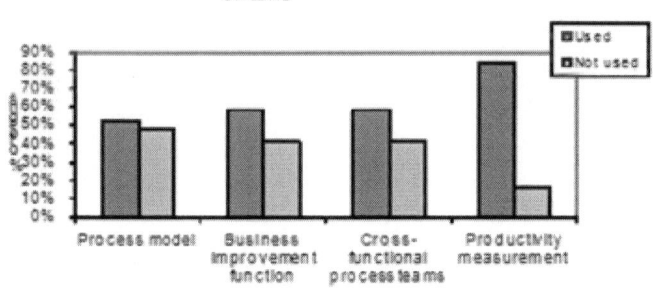

57

The final question asked whether the respondents believed that there would be an increase in the use of activity and process information in their organisation. All but two of the 31 respondents, including the four who had not yet considered the development of activity based information, agreed that there would be an increase. One of the two 'dissenters' said *No* because they did not believe that they could use it more than they were doing at the moment!

5.5 Key Findings

The absence of a visible link between ABM and a defined process framework is one of the reasons suggested by a number of people involved in its development in Lloyds TSB for the failure of ABM to realise its potential of providing both cost and service information to enable process improvement opportunities to be identified. One of the objectives of the research was to identify whether a process background had influenced the use and benefits of activity based information. Further analysis of the base data was undertaken to address this objective.

There was an almost even split in the 31 replies between organisations with and without a process model (16/15). This criteria was used to identify the influence on the type of benefits claimed from the use of activity based information. Of the 16 organisations with a process model, 15 used or were planning to use activity based information; 12 of the 15 without a process model were in the same position. Figure 5.7 presents a comparison of the benefits, achieved or expected, claimed by these organisations.

A significantly higher proportion of those organisations with a process model claimed each of the benefits, and the difference is more noticeable as the chart moves from cost towards process and customer service benefits. Of the 18 organisations claiming improved customer service as one of the benefits of activity based information, 14 had established a process model.

Organisations with a process model are more likely to have other aspects of what might be considered as components of a process framework. 75% of those with a process model have also established teams responsible for the management of cross-functional processes. This compares with 40% of those without a process model.

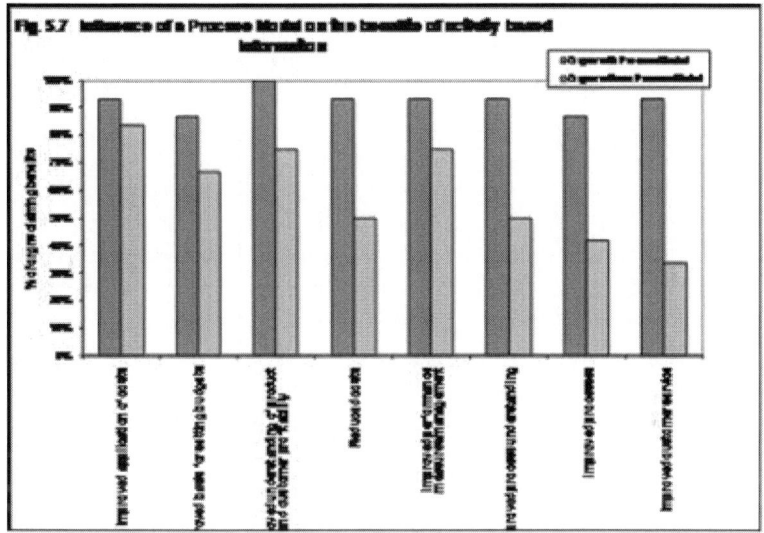

Comment was made in 5.3 about the establishment of a budget to support development and implementation. The proportion of 'process' organisations with a budget was more than three times as many as those without a process model – 57% compared with 17%.

5.6 Supplementary Comments

A number of respondents included additional comments on the questionnaire, most relating to the use of activity based information to enable improved cost information. However, several identified problems in exploiting the improvement potential following the initial development and production of the information. The issues identified by many of these respondents are summed up in this comment:

'Initial implementation was costly and difficult to resource without additional people. Although some benefits were gained, the full anticipated benefits were not fulfilled. A structured approach has been abandoned, but I personally believe there is now an even greater need for it.'

Others identified problems in maintaining progress after the person responsible for driving the programme forward left the organisation. Two respondents stated that they had found it difficult to identify and learn from similar organisations applying activity based information for benchmarking purposes. One comment captured the issues surrounding the purpose and use of the various techniques and acronyms:

'ABC and ABM seem to mean different things to different organisations. Whilst the fundamentals of the techniques may be similar, there are a multitude of directions the actual development can take and a variety of purposes to which they can be applied. It has been difficult trying to gain consistent information about these techniques to decide which will best suit our requirements'.

A discussion of these results, and the implications for the development of activity based information to enable improved process management, is provided in the following chapter.

CHAPTER 6
Requirements and Implications: Discussion of the Findings

6.1 Introduction
This chapter provides a discussion of the results from the research. It addresses the research objectives which were to identify the extent to which organisations are using activity based techniques; to identify the development of the techniques in terms of the main drivers and structure; and to establish if there is a link between an organisation's use of activity based techniques for improvement purposes and the use of other process performance tools.

The structure of this chapter reflects the previous one in that comments are made on the findings from each section of the questionnaire, addressing the first two research objectives, followed by a discussion on the key findings which relate to the influence of organisational background on the use of activity based techniques. There is then a reflection on the importance of the research findings, both in supporting and adding to existing literature, and in its implications for the development of ABM in Lloyds TSB.

6.2 The Use of Activity Based Techniques
The first requirement in discussing any concept is in understanding its meaning and purpose. Although the research identified an almost unanimous belief that there would be an increase in the use of activity and process information, there were discrepancies in definition and application. This creates problems in the development of activity based information as organisations find it difficult to identify similar organisations from which to learn and share experiences.

It is not surprising that ABC is the dominant technique used. As well as being the subject of many publications and conferences, it is the basis on which other related techniques tend to be built. Most organisations understand ABC, recognising that it is a technique used to provide more accurate and consistent financial management information, particularly on product and customer profitability. Not surprisingly this was identified in the research as the prime purpose of using activity based information.

As other acronyms such as ABM come into play, the picture is less clear. The definitions provided by those organisations using ABM (and only one-third had a definition of what it entailed) all referred to it as being an extension of ABC data to identify and drive business improvement opportunities and decisions. However, follow-up discussions identified that the emphasis was very much on financial management improvements and decisions relating to product and customer profitability. This contrasts with the specific definition of ABM within Lloyds TSB, which refers to the management of activities to deliver cost and service improvements. The definition positions ABM as a tool for understanding the context of the identified activities and as an integral part of process management.

The emphasis on the financial aspects was reiterated in the benefits achieved or expected through the use of activity based information. In many cases, although providing increased understanding, the information had not necessarily succeeded in driving the action and changes required to deliver the hard benefits in terms of reduced costs, improved processes and customer service. This was not necessarily seen as a failure by most of the organisations, as it was not a prime objective or purpose of their use of activity based information, the focus being on improved financial information. For Lloyds TSB it was an issue, as the role of ABM was as a tool to deliver business improvement.

As the need for activity based information becomes wider in scope, the infrastructure required to support its objectives become more important. The use of the information to deliver change within the organisation means that it becomes subject to the same requirements and principles of other change management programmes, such as leadership from the top, team working, commitment and involvement at all levels, and an understanding of the cultural issues which determine resistance to change (Beckard & Pritchard 1968). These requirements are critical in the development of an ABM that encompasses an extended definition relating to business improvement.

6.3 The Development of Activity Based Techniques

The influence of Finance and the requirement for improved financial information dominated the factors relevant to the development of activity based information. The pivotal role of Finance staff in initiating and progressing the development was evident in the vast majority of the replies. It was therefore not surprising that the focus for organisations in this research was on ABC aspects rather than the wider scope provided by the extended definition of ABM.

In discussions with a consultant who had been involved with the implementation of about 40 activity based information projects, he stated that the vast majority were simply for financial management purposes. He believed that the extension of the purpose to cover improvement activity was usually initiated by a consultant and was dependent on their involvement at the planning stage. These comments were consolidated to an extent by this research, where the purpose was more likely to include reference to improvement activity when external consultants were involved on the Project Team.

It was interesting to see the level of constraints facing implementation. Most of the organisations implementing activity based information indicated one or more issues which affected development. The pressures on organisations in a rapidly changing environment mean that there are many competing initiatives for a limited pot of resource and money, all needing to be implemented as quickly as possible. However, without the commitment and resources, the full potential of the initiative is often sacrificed to expediency, with implementation restricted to what can be delivered quickly rather than what is required to meet the original identified objectives. To a large extent, this was the dilemma facing implementation of ABM in Lloyds TSB and is a significant factor contributing to its perceived failure to deliver the level of benefits anticipated at its initiation.

6.4 Organisational Background

The information on organisational background, in terms of the use of other process performance tools, was required to identify if this played a part in the use and benefits of activity based management. As 84% of the organisations had implemented other recognised improvement programmes such as TQM and Continuous Improvement, it could be argued that the use of activity based information for improvement purposes would be simply a duplication of these other initiatives.

However, each initiative serves a different purpose and the key factor is in defining this discrete requirement, while at the same time identifying that they can be integrated into a suite of tools to hopefully add even greater value than the sum of its parts. ABM can be used alongside other performance management and measurement frameworks such as the Balanced Scorecard and the EFQM Business Excellence Framework as each delivers specific information relevant to its defined purpose. It can also be used to identify process improvement requirements and opportunities, which in turn can be delivered through TQM and continuous improvement techniques. There does not have to be only one initiative, but without the necessary understanding and commitment, it is usually easier than developing a suite of tools. The question that organisations will increasingly face as they search for competitive advantage is whether they can afford not to exploit the potential that a variety of tools offer.

All of the tools selected need to be part of an integrated management system which aligns operational activities to corporate strategic objectives. Increasingly the need is to align resources so that teams can see a direct relationship between what they do and the overall corporate strategic goals (Mintzberg 1994).

The growing importance of a clearly defined and communicated strategy has assisted the growth of interest in process management and the tools available to support the approach. Just over half of the organisations in the study had established a process model and teams to manage cross-functional processes. The absence of a process framework, which had underpinned the ABM approach in its development in TSB, was considered to be another key factor in the failure of ABM to embed itself in the culture of Lloyds TSB.

6.5 Key Findings
The impact of a process perspective on the benefits anticipated through the use of activity based information was the key finding in the

research. The results presented in section 5.5 highlight the significant difference between organisations with and without a process model on the scope of identified benefits. Although many of the benefits, particularly the hard benefits as discussed in 6.2 above, were expected rather than already achieved, the presence of a process model indicates a different approach and perspective on the purpose of activity based information.

The potential use of the information to enable delivery of improved processes and customer service in addition to the basic benefits associated with ABC suggests more proactive activity management. In effect it is this that could be said to be one of the factors determining the use of ABM.

6.6 The Importance of the Research Findings

The need for a clearer understanding of the requirements for ABM is reinforced by the fact that 96% of the people who replied to the questionnaire believe that their organisations will make increased use of activity and process information. To enable delivery of the benefits required to allow progress towards achievement of their strategic objectives, organisations need to take advantage of relevant tools and techniques that will assist them in their journey.

One of the major issues identified is the confusion over the use of terminology and purpose of the techniques. Although the purpose and principles of ABC are largely understood, the understanding of ABM varies greatly. Many conferences promise discussion of ABM but talk mainly of ABC. The use of the term Activity Based Cost Management (ABCM), described by Develin & Bellis-Jones (1995), is probably the best term for what many people think of as ABM, namely the use of ABC data to enable improved financial management decisions.

The previous paragraph reflects the confusion surrounding the different terms! Without a consistent understanding of terminology, techniques and purpose, organisations have found it difficult to identify and share relevant information. In many ways the confusion is similar to that caused by the plethora of acronyms and terms describing various fields of business process management. The main difference between the two situations is that within the process literature there was a general consistency in understanding of purpose, and most of the terms were shade differences. ABM, given its full rein, is significantly different in scope from ABC.

By identifying and reporting on activities that make up the critical processes, the information provided is likely to be more relevant to the business than much of the activity based reporting which tends to be created from existing available measurement and allocation. However, this requires an understanding of the critical processes. As these tend to cut across functions, identification of the processes and activities requires additional cooperation, and in many cases a change in culture, which has been identified by many writers including Kaplan (1995) and Cooper (1996) as being one of the most difficult factors to deliver.

The potential of ABM, in setting activities within a process context and providing both cost and service information to identify improvement opportunities, has not been widely discussed in books and journals. This research identifies the link between activity based information and a process perspective, and suggests that the link needs to be firmly established if organisations are to achieve the benefits required.

6.7 The Implications for Lloyds TSB

In many ways, the development of ABM within TSB was impeded by the merger with Lloyds at the end of 1995. The pitfalls identified by Player & Keys (1995) in terms of implementing a pilot ABM programme had been largely addressed: the infrastructure was in place to support ABM; there was commitment from senior executives and the resource to implement the structured programme; there was significant process understanding; teams were established to both manage and reengineer cross-functional processes; the required holistic cost and service information on the performance of the processes and their component activities had been defined. The requirements for ABM, in terms of both purpose and the factors that enable successful implementation, had been clearly identified and were largely being met. However, the momentum that had been built up was halted as new structures and priorities were defined.

The relaunch in Lloyds TSB, although benefiting from increased experience and an enhanced methodology, did not have the same infrastructure to support its implementation. A defined process framework was not widely communicated and there was little understanding of the components of the critical cross-functional processes which delivered to the end customer - the focus was on the pieces of the jigsaw rather than the complete picture; commitment to the programme was not as obvious; and the development became increasingly tailored to provide information to meet financial management requirements. The ABM programme was, to an extent, delivering a more sophisticated version of ABC.

This dilution of purpose means that the potential benefits of ABM are unlikely to be exploited. The use of ABM to enable proactive management of activities to deliver improved processes, reduced costs and improved customer service requires the necessary infrastructure. The results from this research, together with key findings from the literature review, confirm the thoughts of many of the staff involved in the development of ABM. The question is whether the implications of the research will be addressed.

There is undoubtedly a need to do so. Financial services organisations face constant change through increasing competition and increasing awareness in the customer base. A move towards a process based approach as a means to deliver the required changes means that the impact will be on more areas, more profoundly, and more often, than previously. This in turn leads to a requirement for the provision of relevant, business-led, management information that can be used to drive decision making. ABM, by delivering cost and service data on activities and processes, offers the information and understanding required to drive improvement.

6.8 Conclusions
The purpose of this dissertation was to gain an understanding of the requirements for successful ABM. The fact that the vast majority of organisations envisage an increasing use of activity and process information highlights the need for a consistent understanding of the

purpose of the various activity based techniques and the factors enabling successful delivery.

The potential of an extended version of ABM, delivering activity cost and service information to drive process improvements, has not been exploited. This dissertation, however, has identified the factors that will enable successful delivery and has confirmed that the approach originally developed in TSB met the requirements to a significant extent. Although increased experience and an enhanced methodology should have provided a stronger platform for Lloyds TSB to have built on this original development, the lack of many of the components of the supporting infrastructure has led to what, with the glorious benefit of hindsight, may be considered as an inevitable failure in terms of delivering the anticipated high profile benefits.

The key component identified was a process framework to drive the focus of the information on the business critical processes rather than simply a replication of other performance management tools. By identifying the context in which the activities are carried out, and providing information on both cost and service aspects of the individual activities and the resultant process, ABM can complement other process and performance tools.

Many organisations commit to the implementation of one tool only. A clearer understanding of the purpose of the various tools and techniques will enable organisations to more fully exploit the potential that each of them has to offer and enable improved management and delivery of benefits.

CHAPTER 7
Post-Script: The Potential for Further Research

7.1 Limitations of the Research

Although the research delivered a number of significant basic findings, its limitations also need to be considered. The main issue was that the sample was relatively small and quite specific in terms of its population. Potential respondents were identified from a database comprising people who had expressed an interest in ABM and from organisations recognised as having a successful process background. It could therefore be reasonably argued that the results are not necessarily representative of organisations in general.

Although an acceptable percentage of the issued questionnaires were returned, analysis was only based on 31 replies. This meant that more detailed breakdown of the results, for example by industrial classification and by the variables identified in each of the questions, was not feasible as the individual numbers were too small. The potential findings from each of the smaller samples would have produced outputs from which significant differences and implications would have been difficult to justify.

There was also difficulty experienced by some respondents in the terminology used in the questionnaire. In part this reflects the lack of clarification that is evident in the literature, but further testing of the questionnaire with personnel from outside Lloyds TSB before it was issued could have reduced the impact.

7.2 Building on the Experience

The limitations have the effect of positioning the research as a significant pilot study. It has provided a focus on the issues surrounding implementation of ABM from which further research can be developed to address the key requirements.

There are three main factors that need to be built in to this further research. The first is to cover a larger and more diverse population with the questionnaire. This will enable the second requirement of more detailed analysis of the key criteria, which should deliver more robust findings. Finally, the questionnaire needs specifically to address some of the findings from this research, in particular the link between activity based information and process understanding and improvement. This will help to further understand the key factors required to enable successful implementation of ABM or similar initiatives.

The questionnaire should be supplemented by a number of in-depth interviews to draw out further detail and explanation of the responses. The follow-up discussions carried out as part of my research generated a number of valuable comments and interest. The proposed approach for the further research is likely to generate more significant issues which, together with the results from the questionnaire, should serve to further enhance the understanding of the requirements for activity based management.

REFERENCES

ANTOS, J. (1992) 'Activity Based Management for Service, Not-for-Profit, and Governmental Organisations', Journal of Cost Management, Summer, pp.13-24.

ARGYRIS, C. and KAPLAN, R.S. (1994) 'Implementing New Knowledge: The Case of Activity Based Costing', Accounting Horizons, September, pp.83-105.

BECKARD, R. and PRITCHARD, W. (1968) Changing the Essence: the Art of Creating Fundamental Change in Organisations, San Francisco: Jossey Bass Publishers.

BORJESSON, S. (1994) 'What Kind of Activity Based Information Does Your Purpose Require?', International Journal of Operations & Production Management, 14:12, pp.23-42.

BRINKER, B. (ed) (1993) Emerging Practices in Cost Management, Boston: Warren, Gorham & Lamont.

BUSINESS INTELLIGENCE (1994) Reengineering: the Critical Success Factors, London: Management Publications.

COKINS, G. (1996) Activity Based Cost Management: Making It Work, Chicago: Irwin Professional Publishing.

COOPER, R. (1996) 'The Changing Practice of Management Accounting', Management Accounting, March, pp.26-33.

COOPER, R. & KAPLAN. R.S. (1991) The Design of Cost Management Systems, New York: Prentice Hall International.

DAVENPORT, T.H. (1993) Process Innovation, Boston: Harvard Business School Press.

DEVELIN, N. & BELLIS-JONES, R. (1995) No Customer-No Business: The True Value of Activity Based Cost Management, Milton Keynes: Accountancy Books.

GARVIN, D. (1993) 'Building a Learning Organisation', Harvard Business Review, July/August.

GREENWOOD, T.G. and REEVE, J.M. (1992) 'Activity Based Cost Management for Continuous Improvement: A Process Design Framework', Journal of Cost Management, Winter, pp.43-57.

HAMMER, M. (1990) 'Re-engineering Work: Don't Automate, Obliterate', Harvard Business Review, July-August, pp. 104-112.

HAMMER, M. and CHAMPY, J. (1993) Re-engineering the Corporation, New York: HarperCollins.

HAMMER, M. & STANTON, S.A. (1995) The Reengineering Revolution: The Handbook, London: HarperCollinsPublishers.

HAMMER, M. (1996) Beyond Reengineering, New York: HarperCollinsBusiness.

HARRINGTON, H.J. (1991) Business Process Improvement, New York: McGraw Hill.

HARRINGTON, H.J. (1998) 'Performance Improvement: The Rise and Fall of Re-engineering', TQM Magazine, 10:2, pp.69-71.

HIXON, M. (1995) 'Activity Based Management: Its Purpose and Benefits', Management Accounting, June, pp.27-30.

HOWARD, R. (1993) 'ABM Information - TQM's Missing Link', CMA Magazine, March, pp.7-14.

HUFFMAN, J.L. (1997) 'The four Re's of Total Improvement', Quality Progress, 30:1, pp.83-88.

JOHNSON, H.T. (1988) 'Activity Based Information: A Blueprint for World Class Management Accounting', Management Accounting, June, pp.23-30.

JOHNSON, H.T. & KAPLAN, R.S. (1987) Relevance Lost: The Rise and Fall of Management Accounting, Cambridge MA: Harvard Business School Press.

JOHNSON, & SCHOLES, (1993) Exploring Corporate Strategy: Text and Cases, New York: Prentice Hall.

JOHANNSEN, R. & PAGE, J. (1995) The International Dictionary of Management, (5th edn) London: Kogan Page.

KAPLAN, R.S. (1996) 'New Roles for Management Accountants', Journal of Cost Management, Fall, pp.6-13.

KERSHAW, R. and MAHENTHIRAN, S. (1998) 'Business Process Change and the Role of the Management Accountant', Journal of Cost Management, March/April, pp.25-33.

LAMBERT, D. and WHITWORTH, J. (1996) 'How ABC Can Help Service Organisations', CMA Magazine, May, 70:4, pp.24-28.

LEE, R. G. and DALE, B.G. (1998) 'Business Process Management: A Review and Evaluation', Business Process Management Journal, 4:3, pp.27-32.

LETZA, S.R. and GADD, K. (1994) 'Should Activity Based Costing Be Considered as the Costing Method of Choice for Total Quality Organisations?', TQM Magazine, 6:5, pp.27-42.

MILLER, J. A. (1992) 'Designing and Implementing a New Cost Management System', Journal of Cost Management for the Manufacturing Industry, Winter, pp.41-54.

MINTZBERG, H. (1994) 'The Fall and Rise of Strategic Planning', Harvard Business Review, January-February, pp.13-26.

PLAYER, R.S. and KEYS, D.E. (1995) 'Lessons from the ABM Battlefield', Journal of Cost Management, Spring, pp.26-39; Summer, pp.20-36; Fall, pp.31-42.

PLOWMAN, B. (1997) 'The Cost of the Customer', TQM Magazine, 9:1, pp.54-60.

PORTER, M.E. (1985) Competitive Advantage, New York: The Free Press.

SAUNDERS, M., LEWIS, P., and THORNHILL, A. (1997) Research Methods for Business Students, London: Pitman Publishing.

SMEDS, R. (1996) 'Successful Transformation: Strategic Evolution Management for Competitive Advantage', Business Change and Reengineering, 3:2, pp.33-42.

STORAGE TECHNOLOGY CORPORATION (1996) ABC / ABM Tutor, [online] [cited 23 June 1998] Available from Internet <URL:http://www.stortek.com>

TURNEY, P.B. (1996) Activity Based Costing: the Performance Breakthrough, London: Kogan Page.

WARNER, M. (ed) (1997) The Concise International Encyclopaedia of Business and Management, London: Thomson Business Press.

ZAIRI, M. (1997) 'Business Process Management: A Boundaryless Approach to Modern Competitiveness', Business Process Management Journal, 3:1, pp.64-80.

APPENDIX 1
The Questionnaire

Dear

I am researching the extent to which organisations are using, or considering the use of, activity based techniques for costing and improvement purposes, and in particular the application of Activity Based Management. This will contribute to my dissertation, the final part of a MSc in Business Process Management course carried out through Sheffield Business School, part of Sheffield Hallam University.

I am writing to you as you have expressed an interest in ABM through the CIMA Contacts Register. I would be grateful if you could complete the enclosed questionnaire, which should take about 20 minutes to complete. Any additional comments will be gratefully received, as would the opportunity to discuss your answers. If you or one of your colleagues would be willing to talk about the replies in more detail, or any aspects of this research, please complete the relevant information on the final page.

At this stage, I must let you know that away from my studies I am a Project Manager with Lloyds TSB. However, please be sure that all information that you provide will be treated in confidence and will not be disclosed to anyone else in Lloyds TSB. You do not need to put your details on the questionnaire, but it would help me if you did. The most important aspect however is to receive information on the application of activity based techniques.

I would be grateful if you could return the questionnaire by Wednesday 18th November, although an earlier return would be greatly appreciated. A stamped addressed envelope is enclosed. I will of course be happy to send you details of my findings, and to discuss any other aspects of my research. Please let me know if you would like any further information. In the meantime, thank you for your time in reading this, and I hope you enjoy the questionnaire.

ACTIVITY BASED MANAGEMENT QUESTIONNAIRE
The extent to which organisations are using ABM

Please tick appropriate boxes or comment in the spaces provided.

> **Section 1: the use of activity based techniques**

Throughout this section, the term 'activity based information/techniques' can mean ABC, ABM, ABCM, or other variation.

1. Does your organisation use activity based information?
   Yes ☐   No ☐   ***If "yes" go to question 4***

2. If not, is your organisation considering its use?
   Yes ☐   No ☐   ***If "no" go to question 21***

3. If considering using activity based information, at what stage is your organisation?
   Information gathering ☐
   Evaluating ☐
   Planning implementation ☐

4. Which of the following does your organisation use to describe the techniques used or planned?
   (Please tick more than one box if appropriate)
   ABC   (Activity Based Costing)   ☐
   ABM   (Activity Based Management)   ☐
   ABCM (Activity Based Cost Management)   ☐
   Other - *please describe below*   ☐
   _____

5. If described as ABM, does your organisation have a short definition of what it entails?
   Yes ☐   ***If "yes" please write the definition below***
   No ☐   _____

6. Which of the following phrases <u>best</u> describes the purpose of the activity based information used in your organisation?

The provision of more accurate information on the ☐

The provision of relevant information to enable ☐

7. What benefits have been achieved or are expected through the use of activity based information in your organisation?
   (Please tick all that apply)

	Achieved	Expected
More accurate application of costs	☐	☐
Improved basis for setting budgets	☐	☐
Improved understanding of product/customer profitability	☐	☐
Reduced costs	☐	☐
Improved performance measures and management	☐	☐
Improved understanding of processes	☐	☐
Improved processes	☐	☐
Improved customer service	☐	☐

   Please describe any other significant benefits below

   _____

8. To what extent have activity based techniques been planned or implemented?

	Planned	Implemented
Selected departments	☐	☐
Selected functions / business units	☐	☐
Organisation wide	☐	☐

9. What type of work is covered or is planned to be covered by your activity based technique?

	Planned	Covered
Operational activities	☐	☐
Support activities	☐	☐
Managerial activities	☐	☐

Section 2: the development of activity based techniques

10. What influenced your decision to use or investigate activity based techniques? *(Please tick all that apply)*

    Strategic business objectives ☐
    Requirement for improved financial information ☐
    Requirement to support process understanding ☐
    Published reports of relevant techniques ☐
    Information from conferences ☐
    Information from external consultants ☐

11. Who was the main driver behind the use or investigation of activity based techniques?

    Chief Executive ☐
    Finance Director ☐
    Change Management Director ☐
    Other - *please detail* ☐

---

12. Which of the following have been used in the development of activity based techniques?

    Steering Committee ☐
    Project Team ☐
    External Consultants ☐

13. If used, from which areas were members involved?

	Steering Committee	Project Team
Finance	☐	☐
Sales	☐	☐
Operations	☐	☐
Marketing	☐	☐
Personnel	☐	☐
Change Management	☐	☐
External Consultants	☐	☐
Other - *please detail below*	☐	☐

14. Was the implementation of activity based techniques subject to a structured project plan or formal methodology?
Yes ☐   *If "yes" was it developed internally*   **Int.** ☐
No ☐   *or externally?*   **Ext.** ☐

15. Has the activity based information used existing data or has it required new data to be created?
Existing data ☐   **Both, but mainly existing** ☐
New data required ☐   **Both, but mainly new** ☐

16. Has a separate budget been established to support the development and implementation?
Yes ☐
No ☐

17. Is development and implementation subject to any of the following constraints?
(Please tick all that apply)
Cost ☐
Prioritisation ☐
Time ☐
Commitment ☐
Resource ☐
Technology ☐

18. What analysis or mapping software tools are used to support the activity based techniques?
_____

19. Are the objectives of the activity based information linked to the overall business objectives?
Yes ☐   **No** ☐

20. Have activities been identified from mainly a top down or bottom up basis?
Top down ☐
Bottom up ☐
Both ☐

Section 3: organisation background

21. Has your organisation implemented any of the following programmes or models? *(Please tick all that apply)*
   TQM ☐   Balanced Scorecard ☐
   EFQM / BEM ☐   Executive Information System ☐
   BPR / BPM ☐   Continuous Improvement ☐

22. Have training programmes been established to support the initiatives identified above?
   Yes ☐   *Please underline relevant initiatives in Q 21*
   No ☐

23. Is there an area responsible for business improvement across the organisation?
   Yes ☐   No ☐
   If "yes" what is the area called? _____

24. Has a 'process model' been established for your organisation?
   Yes ☐   No ☐
   If "yes" when was it developed? _____

25. Have teams been established to manage cross-functional processes?
   Yes ☐   No ☐

26. Is productivity measurement established within your organisation?
   Yes ☐   No ☐
   If "yes" which staff are covered by the measurement?
   Operational ☐
   Support ☐
   Managerial ☐

27. Do you consider that there will be an increase in the use of activity and process information in your organisation?
   Yes ☐   No ☐

Other information

Please include any further comments you may have on the use of ABC / ABM in the space below.

Thank you for completing this questionnaire. All information will be treated in confidence, but it will help me if you complete the details below.

Name _____

Organisation _____

Main Business Activity _____

Please tick the box if you would like a summary of the results. ☐

If you or one of your colleagues would be prepared to discuss your answers, please give a contact name and number below.

Name _____

Telephone _____

Please return the questionnaire in the envelope provided by 18th November. If you would like to discuss any aspects of this document or the research, please contact me. Thank you.

APPENDIX 2
Questionnaire Results - Base Data

Section 1: the use of activity based techniques

Q.1. Does your organisation use activity based information?

Base	31	
Yes	22	71%
No	9	29%

Q.2 If not, is your organisation considering its use?

Base	9	
Yes	5	56%
No	4	44%

Q.3 If considering using activity based information, at what stage is your organisation?

Base	5	
Information gathering	4	80%
Evaluating	1	20%
Planning implementation	1	20%

Q.4. Which of the following does your organisation use to describe the techniques used or planned?

Base	26	
ABC	21	81%
ABM	11	42%
ABCM	6	23%
Other	2	8%

Q.5. If described as ABM, does your organisation have a short definition of what it entails?

Base	*11*	
Yes	4	36%
No	7	64%

Q.6. Which of the following phrases best describes the purpose of the activity based information used in your organisation?

Base 26

The provision of more accurate information on the cost and profitability of products and customers	17	66%
The provision of relevant information to enable process improvement activity	5	19%
Both	4	15%

Q.7. What benefits have been achieved or are expected through the use of activity based information in your organisation?

	Achieved		Expected	
Base	*26*		*26*	
More accurate application of costs	15	58%	10	38%
Improved basis for setting budgets	2	8%	19	73%
Improved understanding of product and customer profitability	13	50%	13	50%
Reduced costs	4	15%	17	65%
Improved performance measures	4	15%	20	77%
Improved process understanding	13	50%	7	27%
Improved processes	4	15%	14	54%
Improved customer service	3	11%	15	58%
Other	3	11%	3	11%

Q.8. To what extent have activity based techniques been planned or implemented?

	Planned	Implemented
Base		
Selected departments		
Selected functions / business units		
Organisation wide		

Q.9. What type of work is covered or planned to be covered by your activity based technique?

	Planned	Covered
Base	*26*	*26*
Operational activities	4 15%	20 77%
Support activities	6 23%	18 69%
Managerial activities	8 31%	11 42%

Section 2: the development of activity based techniques

Q.10 What influenced your decision to use or investigate activity based techniques?

Base	26	
Strategic business objectives	14	54%
Requirement for improved financial information	24	92%
Requirement to support process understanding	16	62%
Published reports of relevant techniques	4	15%
Information from conferences	2	8%
Information from external consultants	3	12%

Q.11. Who was the main driver behind the use or investigation of activity based techniques?

Base	24	
Chief Executive	1	4%
Finance Director	17	71%
Change Management Director	2	8%
Other	5	21%

Q.12. Which of the following have been used in the development of activity based techniques?

Base	22	
Steering Committee	9	41%
Project Team	21	95%
External Consultants	9	41%

Q.13. If a Steering Committee or Project Team was established, from which areas were members involved?

	Steering Committee		Project Team	
Base	9		21	
Finance	9	100%	20	95%
Sales	3	33%	6	29%
Operations	8	89%	17	81%
Marketing	2	22%	4	19%
Personnel	2	22%	3	14%
Change Management	2	22%	6	29%
External Consultants	3	33%	8	38%
Other	5	56%	7	33%

Q.14. Was the implementation of activity based techniques subject to a structured project plan or formal methodology?
Base 24
Yes 21 88%
No 3 12%

If yes, was it developed internally or externally?
Base 21
Internally 18 86%
Externally 4 19%

Q.15. Has the activity based information used existing data or has it required new data to be created?
Base 25
Existing data 3 12%
New data required 1 4%
Both, but mainly existing 16 64%
Both, but mainly new 5 20%

Q.16. Has a separate budget been established to support the development and implementation?
Base 26
Yes 10 38%
No 16 62%

Q.17. Is development and implementation subject to any of the following constraints?
Base 25
Cost 13 52%
Time 19 76%
Resource 21 84%
Prioritisation 17 68%
Commitment 14 56%
Technology 10 40%

Q.19 Are the objectives of the activity based information linked to the overall business objectives?

Base	*25*	
Yes	20	80%
No	5	20%

Q.20. Have activities been identified from mainly a top down or bottom up basis?

Base	*25*	
Top down	5	20%
Bottom up	7	28%
Both	13	52%

Section 3: organisation background

Q.21 Has your organisation implemented any of the following programmes or models?

Base	*31*	
TQM	17	53%
EFQM / BEM	9	29%
BPR / BPM	8	26%
Balanced Scorecard	13	42%
Executive Information System	10	32%
Continuous Improvement	19	61%

Q.22 Have training programmes been established to support the initiatives identified above?

Base	*26*	
Yes	20	77%
No	6	23%
TQM	14	70%
EFQM / BEM	7	35%
BPR / BPM	3	15%
Balanced Scorecard	5	25%
Executive Information System	1	5%
Continuous Improvement	14	70%

Q.23 Is there an area responsible for business improvement across the organisation?

Base	*31*	
Yes	18	58%
No	13	42%

Q.24 Has a 'process model' been established for your organisation?

Base	*31*	
Yes	16	52%
No	15	48%

Q.25 Have teams been established to manage cross-functional processes?

Base	*31*	
Yes	18	58%
No	13	42%

Q.26 Is productivity measurement established within your organisation?

Base	*31*	
Yes	26	84%
No	5	16%

If 'yes' which staff are covered by the measurement?

Base	*26*	
Operational	26	100%
Support	12	46%
Managerial	7	27%

Q.27 Do you consider that there will be an increase in the use of activity and process information in your organisation?

Base	*31*	
Yes	29	94%
No	2	6%

APPENDIX 3
Pitfalls in ABM Implementation

The following table outlines the ten pitfalls associated with each of the three stages of an ABM implementation. Although these pitfalls were identified through research carried out by Player and Keys, they reflect and summarise the findings of many other writers who have considered the problems of implementation (as discussed in Chapter 3).

Getting off to the right start	Developing the pilot	Moving from pilot to mainstream
Lack of top-management buy-in	Failure to begin with a pilot	Individual resistance to change
Failure to understand the three views of cost	Too much detail	Departmental resistance to change
Lack of clear objectives	Too little detail	Resistance to changing beliefs and value systems
A financial person heads the ABM project	Problems in collecting activity data	Environmental barriers to change
Lack of employee involvement	Inaccurate assignment of costs	No formal plans to act on ABM information
Lack of funding	Unavailability of data	Lack of clear, concise and easily understandable reports
Lack of training	Costs not assigned to right year	Problems with reporting frequency
"Outside consultants did it to us"	Software problems	ABM not implemented in a profit centre
Lack of expertise	Poor project management	Company is too profitable for ABM
No link between ABM and other management initiatives	People do not have enough time	ABM system is too costly to maintain

Source: Player and Keys (1995)

Back to the Future

A more detailed look at the development of Activity Based Management in TSB

A Guide to ABM

To support the implementation of Activity Based Management in TSB, a guide was developed to provide details of its approach and purpose; the database construction and its contents; and thoughts on how the data could be best utilised. The guide was accessible to all staff who needed to know about ABM, either as data collectors or as information users. So how did it describe ABM back in 1995?

> ABM is a well established measurement tool in manufacturing, having proven the benefit of recording and measuring the ways in which goods are made and delivered to the customer.
>
> By gaining a thorough understanding of the activities that combine to make a process, it is possible to **identify the areas of waste, value added** and **non value added activity** and so develop a programme of **continuous improvement** or radical redesign, focusing upon **customer requirements** and improving **business performance**.
>
> With effective ABM, it is possible to accurately predict the effect of changes in volumes or business mix, or of new product launches, on the company's costs. ABM, which is principally a **Management Information System**, also supports the **budgeting** process, **product profitability** analysis and **customer profitability** analysis.
>
> In the way ABM compares the **cost and value** of an activity, an objective decision can be made as to whether the activity should continue, or where the process requires improvement.
>
> ABM incorporates:
> 1. Activity measurement, e.g. costs, duration, frequency, value
> 2. Service performance, especially in relation to the time taken to get products and services to the customer
> 3. Control of the consumption of resources by the activity
> 4. Management intervention to rectify problem areas
> 5. Continuous improvement of the cost and service performance by eliminating non value added activities and improving efficiency and effectiveness of remaining activities.

TSB believed the use of its particular version of ABM was innovative within the Financial Sector, and an enabler to position the business at the leading edge of process management. This in turn was seen as providing the potential for a clear competitive advantage by being able to accurately quantify various dimensions of the business, to better control costs, and to improve customer service.

TSB's Business Plan in 1992 committed to a programme of **Business Process Re-engineering** to achieve sustainable business benefits through improved customer service and cost reduction. To enable process re-engineering, an understanding and management of the end-to-end processes that delivered customer service was required. The development of a Process Framework allowed a view of the organisation that was different to the traditional functional and product perspectives. Business Process Management (BPM) looked at the business from a process dimension, removing the traditional functional barriers.

In order to record processes for the first time, in what was historically a functionally based company, it was necessary to develop an overall process framework. The **TSB Process Framework** represented all of the Bank's activities in various process categories. The identification and consideration of activities in a process perspective allowed the Bank to focus on performing whole processes well, rather than on optimising separate tasks. Identifying key business processes also enabled the setting of process improvement targets, prioritisation of re-engineering work and, critically, the introduction of process management.

Within TSB, a process was defined as '*a set of activities that result in the creation and delivery of value to the customer*'. The TSB Process Framework took initial high level groupings of activities and broke them down into more detailed processes and sub-processes. The three high level processes of Direction Setting & Control, Customer Facing, and Support were broken down into the 17 generic processes. These in turn were made up of what was known as the 'top 50' processes.

The majority of the work carried out under the banner of Business Process Re-engineering focused on the Customer Facing Processes

(CFPs) since they contained the greatest cost and the potential for greatest customer service improvement. The four generic processes detailed within CFP were broken down into the 17 processes detailed in a Data Definitions document and against which the business process descriptions in the ABM Process Blueprints were coded.

To help the Bank move from the traditional functional perspective towards a process view, the CFPs were grouped into six product aligned processes which were easily recognised and understood by functionally based management. These product related activity sets were Homebuying Services, Insurance Services, Savings & Investment Services, Payment Services, Lending Services, and Commercial.

A process matrix was then developed which recognised both the **generic processes** such as New Business and **the product aligned processes** such as Homebuying Services.

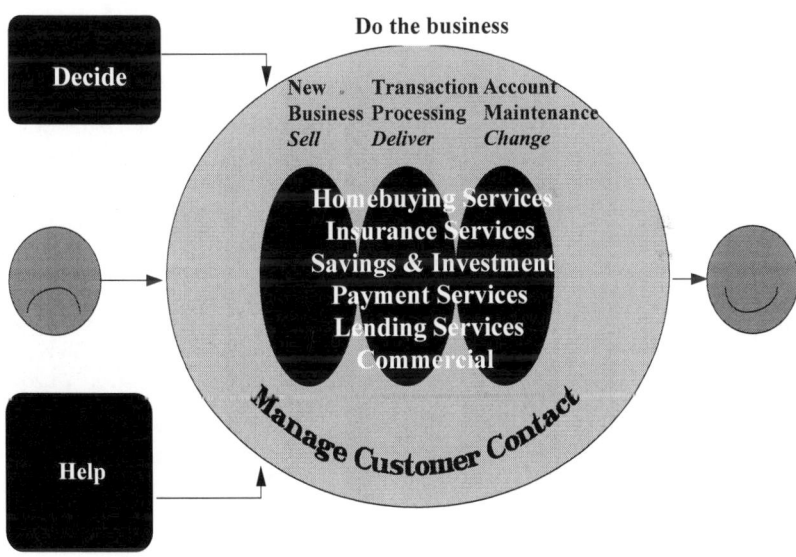

Information had previously been available and provided on a product or department basis, often making it difficult to compile an accurate picture of the whole, customer-to-customer, process where it crossed functional boundaries. To support the process perspective required and provided by BPM, an information system was required which would enable improved management of various dimensions of the key business processes, and identify and prioritise potential improvement opportunities.

Processes were defined and mapped, then further modified to show the commonality of much of the process work - subsequently termed generic process maps. Activity Based Costing was the initial vehicle for the required information, driven centrally rather than by line management, by way of a separate project aimed at costing the maps and their activities. However, the disparity between local business descriptions of their processes and the limited definitions of the process framework meant that there was some uncertainty over the validity and depth of the measurement.

Activity Based Management provided more detailed and wide ranging management information within a framework created out of local business requirements but which fitted with the bank-wide process perspective. ABM enabled understanding and management of the string of activities making up a process, at both a local level through identifying and improving a part of the process, and at Process Owner level in assessing the overall picture, end to end.

The required output from the information to be collected was identified through talking to process and line management. It needed to be in an easily recognisable form in which the whole cost of a process and linkages between activities could be identified, and which would highlight variability and capacity.

The (unique) Common Activity Model
Although the 'product process' perspective provided a means of grouping together a set of activities, it was clear that there was a range of activities, such as *'enter data'*, which existed across the company, and that critical value could be obtained by identifying and comparing the

performance of these activities across the business. In order to do this a Common Activity Model (CAM) was developed to provide a consistent framework for describing activities at all sites within the Bank. This was particularly important since different sites often described the same activity in different ways. The Model acted as a bridge between the local description of a process and the generic descriptions used in the TSB Process Framework. It was described as "The CAMbridge" (very witty at the time!)

The CAM ensured that 'local' site ownership of the data was retained through the use of its own terminology and accepted measurement, but allowed the move towards a process perspective by introducing process language and concepts to traditional functional activity descriptions. By enabling the company to progress a cross functional perspective, the CAM allowed it to seek out the greatest efficiencies in cost and service performance.

The Common Activity Model took each Activity in the Process Description and coded it in terms of **Generic Process**, **Sub-Assembly**, and **Common Activity** ('Common' was used in the sense of 'bank-wide common understanding', e.g. local descriptions of 'Update Customer Details' and 'Update Name & Address' were essentially viewed in the Model as the same common activity.)

The **Generic Process** referred to the descriptions used in the TSB Process Framework outlined above, and detailed in a supporting Data Definitions document. A Customer Facing Process was one which directly contributed to meeting a *Customer Purpose*, a definable and recognisable need which the customer believed can be satisfied by the Bank.

Sub-assemblies were called up or triggered by a customer need, and were essentially a collection of activities undertaken by the Bank. Different sub-assemblies could be grouped together to form a discrete, meaningful process to satisfy the customer's purpose.

A **Common Activity** was a discrete task or action which could be grouped with other specific activities to form a sub-assembly. A common activity could exist in a number of different sub-assemblies and could have different parameters in each. Measurement of resource was usually recorded at this level.

Sometimes we got quite pretentious in trying to describe our work, as in the following analogy that started doing the rounds.

The fish analogy

One fish can join other fish to form a shoal. A number of shoals of fish can group together and take on the outline appearance of an elephant. Each fish, (the Common Activity), is unique. Each fish contributes to their shoal, (the Sub-Assembly), but could equally contribute to another. The shoals do not become an elephant, (the Process), they only look like it.

As with any information system, the CAM did not provide solutions, but it did provide another level of information to enable improved analysis and decisions.

The vehicle for ABM was the **Process Blueprint**, and the core of each Blueprint was the Process Description. This detailed the Sub-Processes which made up the Process, and the Activities which made up each Sub-Process. Against each line of this description were a number of data fields, which were populated to allow report production and analysis.

Some of the data required was coding which allowed identification of each line of the description (such as the *sequence code* and relevant *cost centre*) and which tended to remain constant. Other fields were used to input variable data (such as volumes and timings) which could change with each submission. The responsibility for completing the data fields for each line of the Process Description rested with the data collectors in the function identified by the *source function* code for each line.

The Process Blueprints were described in local business terms to allow for functional understanding and ease of measurement. The CAM added an extra dimension by applying common descriptions which could be recognised throughout the Bank and so enable more detailed analysis of Bank-wide activities. Common descriptions allowed for improved understanding of the overall process perspective which became increasingly important in terms of the Bank realising the benefits of applying Business Process Management.

To enable this improved understanding, each activity in the Blueprint Process Description was mapped to the CAM, i.e. Generic Process code, Sub-Assembly code, and Activity code.

The coding allowed for detailed analysis to be undertaken through the central database, enabling information to be considered at Generic Process, Sub-Assembly, and Activity level. The database could be sliced by any of these dimensions to identify the different types of work being undertaken throughout the Bank. It was now possible to identify where similar activities were carried out, which meant process improvements could be shared across the Bank.

The data fields showed the following elements for each sub-process or activity within an identified blueprint:

- Sequence of sub-processes and activities
- Cost Centre of area carrying out the activity
- Dependent sub-processes
- Whether the sub-process was a standard part of the process
- Distribution channel
- Product code
- Transaction code
- Fit with the Common Activity Model *(Process, Sub-Assembly, Common Activity)*
- Volumes
- Staff Grade
- Work Content
- Elapsed time
- Customer concerns
- Staffing (FTEs)

As the **Customer Facing Processes** were the initial focus of the BPM redesign work and provided the greatest opportunity for improved customer service and cost reduction, the initial ABM process blueprints concentrated on the CFPs.

Each of the sites was asked to identify their major processes and then break them down into ***sub-processes*** and ***activities***, listing them to form a *site process blueprint.* These individual blueprints were combined by the central ABM team to produce *end-to-end process blueprints.*

The sites undertook Pareto analysis (80/20 rule) to identify the most costly processes by FTE staff, describing the activities within the identified processes in their own words and populating the relevant blueprints until ***approximately 80% of their 'customer facing' FTEs were accounted for***, although some variations naturally existed in the early iterations.

Following the identification and validation of the process blueprints, each site was asked to populate their activities on all the relevant blueprints. This included populating activities carried out in blueprints which they may not have originally identified, but which had been detailed by another site as part of their end-to-end process.

The central database was built and maintained by the Productivity Information section, within the Business Improvement structure. The database was constructed using Microsoft Excel together with a multi dimensional enhancing package known as TM1 Perspectives. Flowcharts were constructed using ABC FlowCharter software. And after the initial outputs, work continued to enhance the system by automating the input, developing and refining the output, and responding to Management requirements.

It was intended that the value and use of the ABM data would evolve over time with extended coverage, experience and continuing improvements in data quality.

ABM data could be used at both Process Owner and local level, providing a view of the end to end process and from a local perspective. Analysis provided the opportunity to view a variety of performance information such as unit costs; total elapsed time; trends over time; apportionment of costs across a process; concerns; how much is directly related to delivering to the customer and how much is not, etc.

The greatest potential for cost savings was within the processes that consumed the major share of resources, and ABM was able to provide a clear picture of where staff resource was consumed at process, sub-process and activity levels. The resource requirement obviously varied between processes. At one extreme, high resource requirements could result from a high volume of relatively short cycle tasks, where improvement often called for a more detailed examination of work place layout and clerical routines such as data input and system responses; or they could be the result of relatively infrequent but time consuming activities, which may require an examination of the method being used, e.g. awkward, inappropriate or unnecessary activities. Whatever the problem or cause, ABM data helped to highlight the issue and enable questions to be asked of the right people.

ABM reports provided a very quick and easy method of monitoring initial project savings, by comparing the original and reworked measures, and allowed for continued monitoring to detect potential relapses. Understanding unit costs and the development of business models also allowed improved budgeting and forecasting. Production planning was easily accommodated, with the impact of future options, new products or volume increases more easily measured. Scheduling plans could be maximised by looking across the whole process and the consequent resource management requirements.

So ABM provided a baseline for improved understanding of the organizations processes and costs, describing and quantifying processes in a tangible form, which could then be further worked upon using more conventional techniques.

But as discussed in my dissertation, the potential of ABM was never fully exploited. The first reports were produced in TSB in the same month that the merger with Lloyds was announced – and so our resource was diverted to ensuring some of the practical impact of that marriage was realized as effectively as possible. Later, development of ABM in Lloyds TSB was also interrupted by significant internal organizational changes.

And then the organization embraced Six Sigma and Lean, and very successfully. Look at the thought process behind a value stream map and you can see that the thought process that was the driver for ABM was on the right track.

Activity-based management: the Lloyds TSB experience

An article published in
Management Accounting
Vol 78 Number 03 March 2000

This article was written by Jane Gibbon, Jan Loughran and John Robinson from the University of Northumbria, and Karen Johnston, University of Teesside. But I like to think I had some small part to play in the final version that appeared on page 48 of the magazine for chartered management accountants, between features entitled '*A PC is not just for Christmas, it's for...how long?*' and '*No business without show business*'. Actually, looking through the rest of the contents, the magazine seems to be much more interesting than I naively thought it would be.

The fifth ABM Exchange was hosted in November by Lloyds TSB at their International Services Centre in Birmingham, facilitated by a team from the Universities of Northumbria and Teesside and sponsored by CIMA Technical Services. This article provides an overview of the day, outlining the specific development of activity-based management in Lloyds TSB, and the subsequent issues raised and discussed.

John Bentien of Central Operations welcomed participants and outlined the origins, development and definition of ABM in Lloyds TSB and some of the issues that had been faced at various stages of the programme. This introduction was followed by the first of three short presentations by John to launch the group discussions. The morning session focused on project management, followed by two further sessions in the afternoon on the activity-based system and change management.

Introduction of ABM in Lloyds TSB

The development of ABM was a culmination of other programmes and initiatives, such as total quality management and business process re-engineering that had produced an improvement culture and a process framework focused on the external customer. There was also a recognition that existing activity-based costing work needed to be adapted to support the developing approach to process management. This approach produced an increasing demand for both cost and service information to reflect the processes identified as critical to delivering customer requirements.

The overall objective of the ABM programme was to enable business improvement through improved understanding, information and management of the banks activities and processes. This in turn was seen as a key enabler in supporting Central Operations' mission 'to be the lowest-cost provider in the industry whilst maintaining service quality'. The holistic cost and service information provided by ABM would support the drive to meet one of the key management challenges, informally summarized as, 'any idiot can slash costs, any

107

idiot can improve customer service. The challenge is in doing both at the same time'.

By providing both cost and service information to support a variety of requirements, ABM was seen as more than an extension to ABC. It was primarily a process management tool that enabled improved costings, rather than a costing tool that supported process management. Critically, placing local activities within the wider business context of the defined end-to-end processes provides a stronger foundation for identifying and assessing the impact of potential improvement opportunities.

A number of critical factors were identified for the development of ABM, which included:

- a supporting process model;
- the integration of process measurement information with financial information;
- senior management commitment;
- involvement of line staff to map their processes;
- facilitation by a central team to create the 'big picture' of the end-to-end processes;
- multi-dimensional software and thinking; and
- acceptance that an 80/20 approach in terms of accuracy and coverage was good enough at the start.

The vision of ABM was to populate activities with data from the bottom up, providing costs at activity level but which could be consolidated at a number of other levels. The focus was initially on staff costs, although the structured framework provided by ABM would also enable other costs to be allocated in a more appropriate way than was previously possible. The key difference between ABM and previous ABC work was the provision of both cost and service information to provide a wider perspective of process performance. The project was driven by Process Management teams, with regularly refreshed information seen to be owned by the business and for the business.

The main outputs from the ABM system are Blueprints and Maps which provide a full understanding of operational processes and the means to identify and measure improvement to those processes. The ABM Blueprint describes the process and shows key activity information such as volumes, work content, resource, customer concerns and elapsed time. The information, on an Excel spreadsheet, feeds through to a multi-dimensional database and ABC Flowcharter to produce process flowcharts which show a summary of the resulting calculated information. The blueprints and maps provide information which help to raise questions such as *'Why the delay?'*, *'What do our customers want?'*, *'How can we get rid of this rework?'*. Developing the answers may in turn lead to identification of potential improvements.

Supporting these outputs is a Common Activity Model which is used to compare common activities across the business to identify total cost of defined activities and best practice. The final part of the ABM toolkit is the Support Activity Model, which is used to enable a similar level of understanding and potential improvement for non-operational or business-sustaining areas that tend to have little traditional measurement for their wide range of non-repetitive activities.

John then raised a number of issues which had surfaced during the ABM development, thus opening the debate for the group sessions. These included the definition and purpose of activity-based techniques and the need to differentiate between ABC, ABCM, and ABM; whether ABM is viewed or should be viewed as a process management tool or a costing tool; the need for action to be taken on the information provided; the question of ownership (local or bank-wide); and the level of priority given to ABM against other initiatives.

Project management
John outlined the project management approach to the implementation of ABM in Lloyds TSB, underlying the need to get off to the right start by addressing common project implementation issues such as a lack of top-management buy-in and clear objectives. Other important issues that could create problems if not identified and addressed are potential problems with employee involvement; whether a financial person heads the ABM project; lack of funding, training & expertise; and the

failure to link ABM and other management initiatives. Other issues needed to be addressed in developing a pilot and extending implementation into the wider business.

The ABM project was started within TSB in April 1995, with five staff from the central Business Improvement function and one person from Finance, with equal numbers from the operational areas. In October 1995 the first outputs were achieved and in December 1995 the data was refreshed for the first time. The merger with Lloyds brought a temporary halt to the structured ABM programme, although individual business areas continued to develop and use the information. The project was then initiated within Lloyds TSB in June 1997 with three staff from Central Operations and 1.5 staff from the pilot areas.

ABM used a structured approach:
- identify the processes;
- apply local measurement;
- consolidate the information
- produce reports; and
- use the outputs.

This is supported by four key enablers: commitment (demand, sponsorship and usage), project management and control (direction, co-ordination and resources, process understanding (context, customer focus and common approach) and measurement (existing and new, wider scope, business relevant).

John believed that one of the key elements for successful implementation of ABM was a supporting process framework to initially identify and define the processes, and to provide the context for the activities. Research had shown that there was a significant difference between organizations with and without a process model on the scope and degree of identified benefits.

The question was asked as to whether the ABM system should be viewed as a project or a philosophy. Once the ABM framework has been delivered by the business it is then for the business to enable process understanding and management and should no longer be viewed as a project.

The activity-based system

The costs output from ABM feed into the ABC system to provide a more co-ordinated approach to charging out the costs of Central Operations to other business areas. This need for change came from identified problems associated with inconsistent allocation of costs, gaps in the data, historic core assumptions, a high proportion of non-volume costs and problems with the ability to benchmark performance.

Although ABM only deals directly with staff costs, the information feeds through to Finance and enables a better defined basis for apportioning other costs such as premises and technology. The ABM/ABC link has moved costings within Central Operations from 'arms and legs' allocation to 'joined up thinking'. The costs within the resources model (budgets by cost centres and cost types, and charges in) are driven by the calculated ABM information to defined activities and then to products. The resulting information is used for transfer pricing, budget setting, business cases and tendering.

ABM information tends to be updated and produced on a quarterly basis to identify changes to process performance over time. Other complementary tools such as FLII (First Line Improvement Information system) are used for daily resource management. The cost and service information can be used to monitor progress, identify issues and prioritise improvement opportunities both at a local level and when consolidated by other relevant areas across the business.

The development of ABM and its link to Finance's ABC system has moved forward the provision and accuracy of both process and cost information. Staff costs and FTE data are now based on actual activity timings and volumes; activities are linked to products by processing area; there is improved allocation of direct processing costs and other headcount related costs; detailed analysis of product costs is available; and budget recharges reflect the ABM costings for many products.

Change management
In the final session, John provided examples of the role of ABM in creating cultural change, enabling process improvements, and delivering improved costings. He also raised potential reasons for the failure to exploit the full potential of an ABM system as an introduction to the final group discussion.

This session concluded a successful ABM Exchange day with participants gaining a considerable insight into the Lloyds TSB experience.

Reflection

15 years after the introduction of ABM in TSB,
10 years after my Dissertation,
was it worth it?

Was it worth it? I like to think the answer is YES. But then I would, wouldn't I. Or else this book is simply an attempt at a cathartic response to my years involved with ABM and its variations under any other name. So what have I gained from being involved in the original development of ABM; and from the initial considered review that resulted in my dissertation; and from this current reflection as described in the previous how many pages?

Well, let's start with the last point, and this publication. When I was younger, so much younger than today (*do you find yourself unwittingly using song lyrics when writing/speaking?*), I found a book written by John Benteen and pretended it was by me. Now, with the advent of various companies offering internet-based self-publishing and printing solutions, the opportunity to massage one's ego in this way has become very easy, with the added benefit that you can bypass other people's criticism of your draft until the deed has been done and the book(s) takes pride of place on your shelf. I would rather have written a best-selling novel, but given that I have never been able to think of a plot that hasn't already been thought of, or indeed anything that I think would be remotely interesting to people, then creating a slim book based around an existing piece of work seemed to be the easy option (and if it isn't interesting to others, well....). So if only for some semblance of misguided smug satisfaction for doing something that anyone can do, it has been worthwhile for me in revisiting the work I had done, and the sense of pride I gained, in obtaining my MSc in Business Process Management.

The end qualification wasn't as important as the means to the end. The research and reflection required to develop my dissertation provided an opportunity to consider what we had done well over the years and what else was needed to really establish end exploit the ABM approach and deliverables. The dissertation hopefully presented a reasonably balanced view of what happened, although I was a little wary of using the intentionally contentious term 'inevitable failure' (p67) in describing the roll-out of ABM in Lloyds TSB, and wasn't sure how the Managing Director would react when he asked for a copy (he actually thought it was good ... or perhaps he didn't read it all). What I did take from writing it was a re-affirmation that 'process', with its myriad of emphases and relationships, was the basis from which an organisation could (should?) continue to improve in terms of both its operational management and, most importantly, its customer service.

That re-affirmation was built on the work that was developed in TSB in the early 1990s, where the significant decision was taken to introduce a programme of Business Process Re-Engineering and subsequently to strengthen this approach with ABM, as outlined in chapter 2 of the dissertation. My involvement in various aspects of this work, and in particular the original development of ABM, shaped much of my thinking and approach, and probably moved me from just 'doing a job' towards having a passion about what I do. And for further increasing my enjoyment of my work and presenting me with a number of different opportunities, I will always look back on those times with great fondness (probably too twee a word, but hopefully you will understand what I mean).

Looking back on what I did learn from the development of ABM, a couple of obvious things stand out. The first is the need to ensure all measures are informed by an understanding of the connected activities within the defined end to end processes; the second is that although the drive towards process management should be provided by senior leaders, the momentum comes from the people who are doing the work and are affected by the need to change.

This was shown as we introduced ABM to the Cheque Clearing department in London, and in particular to the Night Clearing teams. The general view was that they wouldn't be interested – it really was 'just a job'. The advantage was that, at Lloyds TSB, there was a culture of measurement, so these teams were used to being subject to productivity analysis although they tended to just accept whatever came out.

We approached any roll-out with a personal presentation to the team, explaining what we were trying to do and how we thought it could help them. We then followed this by putting all the measured activities and timings from each of the four teams involved in the overall process on individual post-its and placed these on a couple of tables in the centre of the room. We then asked the staff, a couple of people from each team, to put them in a logical order on the wall. Thirty minutes later, there was the outline of an end-to-end process, with clear identification of the hand-offs between teams within an identified timeframe. And significantly, there was effective discussion between the teams, sometimes starting along the lines of *"You cause me right problems with the way you send stuff to us…"*, but ending with an improved understanding of requirements and suggestions about possible improvements. The opportunity to see what happens upstream and downstream allowed people to see the impact of what they were doing. Within four weeks, significant changes had been made to the process following these staff suggestions, with a positive impact on productivity and service delivery. And continuous improvement became slightly more a way of life for these teams. Basic, yes. But effective.

As we rolled out ABM to other departments, similar stories developed. There was ownership within the teams, and greater confidence that the measurement was more robust so that the impact of potential changes, such as process improvements and anticipated increased volumes from marketing campaigns, could be clearly identified and so better enable clearer decisions.

So ABM gave us an end-to-end process description and related process map. It gave us activity timings and costs, and elapsed times and overall process costs, that could be mapped to products and cost centres. It showed hand-offs and exceptions across the process. It identified resource requirements. It showed the 'value stream' and helped to advance the culture of continuous improvement. So what's not to like?

The thinking behind ABM is still applicable, and as it is largely a collection of practical common sense, it is obvious that it also shares common ground with various other more famous approaches and methodologies. Perhaps we didn't make it structured enough, or go out and brand it in the right way, or get a Consultant to sell the concept to executive management, so it was never going to revolutionise the business world. But we did make a difference in our world, and although there may not be a recognisable ABM legacy, it provided the basis for much of what followed in Lloyds TSB and certainly influenced my approach to process management and all that entails. And I still think it's great!

If you want to discuss any aspects of this book, please feel free to contact me via Linked In. Thank you for your time.

John Bentien

January 2011

Printed in Great Britain
by Amazon.co.uk, Ltd.,
Marston Gate.